Praise for

In the Garden with Billy

Lessons About Life, Love, and Tomatoes

" . . . a warm, delightful and thoughtful story chronicling her friendship with the extraordinary Billy Albertson—the kind of friendship celebrating the best that life, in all its trickery, can offer. Simply put, it is a book of gladness in a world of fret, a writer's gift to people who need the tenderness."

> —Terry Kay, author of *The Book of Marie* and *The Valley of Light*

"Charming and thought provoking...the authoress is caught up in whirlwind of ongoing activities involving not only tomatoes but also baby chicks, dandelion wine, and lots more. Along the way, she is not at all reluctant to speak her mind about topics involving parenting and social issues. Ultimately, it is a book about love and remembrance . . . a compellingly funny and heartfelt memoir."

> —George Ellison, author of *Mountain Passages* and *Blue Ridge Nature Journal*

" . . . a powerful, poignant, and persuasive friendship of a young woman and an old man who finds a common bond in their love of the land. Told with passion and a deft touch, it will stir your soul and restore your faith in mankind."

> —Jim Casada, author of *Fly Fishing in the Great Smoky Mountains National Park*

"Winchester has woven her talent for writing and her relationship with an unusual friend into a beautiful novel that speaks to anyone's heart. As you read this story, open your heart and allow yourself to enter into the garden with Billy. You will be amazed at how he will change you too."

> —Joan Koonce, author of *Integrity in a Box of Chocolates:*
> *Consuming Life's Hardships One Bite at a Time*

"Winchester's talent emerges like the sun rising over Georgia shedding light on the people and places in her heart."

> —Jackie K Cooper, author of *The Sunrise Remembers*

In the Garden with Billy

Lessons about Life, Love, and Tomatoes

To: Marie,

In the Garden with Billy
Lessons about Life, Love, and Tomatoes

Renea Winchester

LITTLE CREEK BOOKS

A division of Mountain Girl Press
Bristol, VA

LITTLE CREEK BOOKS

A division of Mountain Girl Press
Bristol, VA

In the Garden with Billy

Lessons About Life, Love, and Tomatoes

Little Creek Books
Published 2010, 2011
All rights reserved.
Copyright © 2010, 2011

You may contact the publisher at:
Little Creek Books
A Division of Mountain Girl Press
P.O. Box 17013
Bristol, VA 24209-7013
E-mail: publisher@littlecreekbooks.com

Library of Congress Control Number: 2011936108
Winchester, Renea
In the Garden with Billy: Lessons About Life, Love, and Tomatoes/
Renea Winchester
ISBN: 978-0-9843192-5-1
   1. Friendship, Biography 2. Southern States–Social Life and customs 3. Gardening

Front cover photograph credits:
Billy and Renea by Janet Bobeng; bottom left by author;
bottom middle by thecameraseye.com; bottom right, public domain

A Note from the Author

This is a work of nonfiction. Billy Albertson is a real person whose name hasn't been changed. He is a remarkable man and my best friend. My hope is that this book reveals the fun one can have when she befriends a stranger. My time in the garden with Billy has been filled with life lessons, laughter, and love. Older people have much to contribute if we allow them the opportunity. Billy has taught me that everyone's life is exciting and meaningful. Many elderly people across this country have wonderful stories, but no one to share them with. Please make the effort to hear someone's story today.

The animals in this book are real, so their names remain unchanged. However, some names in this book have been changed to protect the privacy of certain individuals. I have described, to the best of my ability, events as they were. What mistakes that remain are mine.

Acknowledgments

Thank you Tammy Robinson Smith of Little Creek Books who believed in this story and patiently answered the many questions I had during the process.

Photos found in this book are from a variety of sources. I am fortunate to know two incredibly gifted photographers: Mike Moeller of The Camera's Eye, and Kelle McEntegart of Kelle Mac Photography. A heartfelt "thank you" to both for allowing me to use the images they captured.

Many people have helped me along this journey. To Billy's daughters, Janet and Denise, and his extended family who welcomed me into their family, you are too kind. I am also lucky to have friends, family, fellow writers and the love of my life who have supported me as I stepped out to achieve this dream. My dear ones, I love you grapes and bananas! To the late Wilma Dykeman, who stood atop a smoky mountain years ago and nudged me into this world of writing, I miss you. And to Terry Kay, your friendship is more precious than gold.

Finally, to Billy, I love you. I guess it's time for me to stop all this writing and get back in the garden.

Dedication

*To you God, my heavenly father,
who places people in my path, then laughs
at what happens next.*

Introduction

It's difficult to say how many times I'd passed Billy Albertson's home before I slowed down and pulled into his driveway. His home, in a way, is easy to overlook. It blends into the landscaped yard of hedge bushes and is hidden behind a fifty-year-old magnolia tree he planted shortly after he built the house. On the other hand, his home stands out as one of the few properties in the area that isn't three-stories, covered in three-side-brick, with a three hundred thousand dollar price tag.

One gloomy winter afternoon, I saw signs of life while driving past the house. For a moment I thought the house was on fire. Smoke billowed across the busy two-lane road and filled my nose with a smell I had almost forgotten, smoke from a wood-burning stove. I glanced at the house and smiled. Not many people heat with wood anymore; especially not in Atlanta. As my car punched through the grayness, the oak-smell reminded me of a simpler time.

As the months became years, I passed this home many times while dashing to and from errands. I was always busy, and paid little attention to the single-level brick rancher, until one hot summer day. That was the day my daughter saw a paper plate attached to a rough wooden stick with the words "baby goats 4 sale" scratched in black letters.

Chapter One

Simple Man

"Feel free to stop by anytime."
—Billy Albertson

Billy Albertson wore pale blue overalls patched at the knee. Unbuttoned shirtsleeves flapped as he sped across the carport with a stooped-over gait that was a combination sygoggle shuffle and lope. A frayed hat shielded his face from the sun. Bent pieces of straw had unraveled from the brim and cast haphazard shadows across his cheeks. He ignored the sweat trickling down his face and greeted each customer by name. He bore a striking resemblance to Doreen Cronin's character Farmer Brown in *Click Clack Moo, Cows That Type*. Since our first meeting I have often wondered if Billy was the inspiration for illustrator Betsy Lewin, but I digress.

I met Billy Albertson during the summer of 2008. I had lived in an Atlanta suburb for seven years and had rushed by his house several times a week, ignoring the makeshift signs in his yard: "Goats 4 Sale, Tomatoes, Corn, Firewood . . . " a new sign depending on the season.

I had taken leave from my job to spend time with my mother whose ovarian cancer had returned with a vengeance. She and my father live in the mountains of western North Carolina, and the four hour drive every weekend from Atlanta to their home was taking its toll, as was taxiing my daughter Jamie to and from her summer activities. Then in one of those "yes" moments, I filled the only free time in my schedule by volunteering to serve as Mission Leader during vacation Bible school.

Like most people, I avoid public speaking. Speaking to adults is intimidating, and now I had been assigned the task of teaching the youth. Teaching children ages two to ten-years-old is an exhausting task that gives new meaning to the term "herding cats." As Jamie and I returned

3

from Bible school she saw the "Goats 4 Sale" sign scribbled in black letters on the back of a styrofoam plate and begged me to stop.

"There's always a sign out there that says goats for sale," I argued. I had spent all day teaching hyperactive children about Jesus. I was exhausted and wanted a nap. Stopping to see (and smell) goats in the sweltering sauna of summer wasn't a priority.

"But Mom, this time there's an extra sign on the top that says 'baby.' He has baby goats!" Jamie said.

She loves animals so I relented.

Much like Farmer Brown, Farmer Billy had a problem. Eager customers grabbed tomatoes and tossed money into a small metal barrel. Cars clogged the driveway. In an effort to encourage traffic flow efficiently, he'd fashioned another sign from a plate and nailed it to a wooden post. The sign had the word "tree" written in the middle and a circle drawn around the word. As customers backed out of the drive, Billy waved his arms in the air, pointed to the sign and yelled, "Don't back up . . . just pull forward and circle the tree!"

He was having what I call a "hair on fire moment." Looking at the sweat trickling from his brow he also needed a drink of water.

After waiting patiently for three customers to pay for vegetables, I stepped forward while pointing to Jamie and said, "She's here to see the baby goats."

"My name is Billy," he said, and extended his hand.

He squeezed my hand as I said, "This is Jamie. I'm Renea, but my friends call me Zippy."

Billy's pale blue eyes sparkled with life. He smiled, providing me a glimpse of a soul pure and without guile. "Zzzzzippy," he said with gusto. "I like that name."

He released my hand, opened a plastic bag, and plucked tomatoes from the table. "Goats are out back." He said with a nod, and continued to fill the bag then placed it on a scale which hung from the ceiling of the carport. "Just step behind the house and have a look."

Jamie and I walked behind his 1960s brick home and into another world. Directly in front of us baby chicks scratched in the dirt. They were nestled safely inside a coop made of crumpled tin, chicken wire, and discarded cardboard boxes. To the right, a larger lot held approximately thirty chickens of every size and color imaginable. Behind that structure, four wheelbarrows piled high with tomatoes were waiting to be sold to the long line of customers. Two black and white colored Feist dogs (a breed that resembles Jack Russell Terriers), yapped a greeting. Further back, a chain-link fence protected the garden from twenty or possibly thirty goats. In the garden, row upon row of tomato plants hung bent and burdened.

Jamie was thrilled. She was born an animal lover. Her beautiful freckled face still bears a scar from a cat scratch. Temporary pain doesn't deter her from loving every animal she encounters. Her bravery concerns me. As she boldly approached the goats, I prayed her next scar wouldn't come from a goat's horn.

She immediately asked, "Mom, can I have a goat?"

I hear the, "Mom, can I have a . . . " question each time she is around any animal. "Mom, can I have a rabbit; Mom, can I have an iguana, tarantula, a boa constrictor?" She will repeat this question in the, "are we there yet?" tone until a firm, "No!" is issued by me. Of course she understood that goats would be prohibited on our small lot, so her question quickly became, "Mom, can I have a chicken?"

Since I was wilting, and Jamie was wearing her good shoes, I promised we'd return the following day if only she would let me go home now. As we were leaving we stopped to thank our host.

Billy was hunched over a sagging table loaded with ripe tomatoes. "I'm a little busy now with these here tow-maters," he apologized. "But you stop by here anytime you want and see the goats."

Jamie beamed at the open invitation.

"Looks like you need some helpers in the field," I said.

Billy nodded slightly, and focused on his task. "I've got some family coming in this weekend to help," he said.

It was Monday.

Sometimes, parents don't give children the credit they deserve. As we were leaving Jamie said, "Mom, I want to come back and help Billy after we get some lunch."

"That's nice honey, but you have a tennis lesson this afternoon," I said as I pulled out of the drive.

She thought for a moment. I could almost hear the wheels turning. A smile crossed her face. Most parents recognize the look she gave me. You know the one; it's the smile that emerges the moment your child realizes you can't say no to their request.

"Today's Bible school lesson was about being obedient," she said. "I think God wants us to help Billy instead of me going to tennis."

That afternoon beneath the hot Georgia sun, Jamie and I began a blessed friendship with a remarkable man. We became Billy's garden helpers. During the summer we returned at least three, sometimes four days a week. We toiled beneath an unforgiving sun. We picked crops, were stung by bees, pecked by chickens, and chased by goats. The work ripped our fingernails while the sun blistered our shoulders. Through it all I never imagined how Billy's friendship could change my life.

Chapter Two

Tomatoes $5.00 A Bag

"Around here, folk love their tow-maters."
—Billy Albertson

Tomatoes are Billy's main crop. The summer of 2008 provided Georgia's commercial tomato farmers the perfect growing season. The weather was hot and dry. Rain, though sparse, seemed to fall exactly when needed. Fields hung heavy with swollen green globes that were just beginning to turn pink with the promise that this year farmers would turn a profit.

Then came the salmonella scare.

Whispers about salmonella tainting the summer harvest began in late May. By June, the public was in full panic mode. The airwaves were flooded with warnings urging people to avoid tomatoes. At a time when folk should have been enjoying homegrown tomato sandwiches on white bread with Duke's mayo, heavy on the salt with three shakes of pepper please, the Center for Disease Control (CDC) essentially told consumers that eating tomatoes was digestive suicide.

I recall standing in line at the grocery store one Sunday with a bag full of the lovely delicacy when the woman behind me asked, "Don't you know about the tomato scare?"

I nodded and said, "I'm not concerned. I wash my fruits and vegetables before eating them."

What I really wanted to say was, "Honey, didn't your mother teach you the first rule of thumb in any kitchen is effective hand washing? If you apply the same rule to fruits and vegetables you'll be fine." But my mother raised me to be polite.

While people panicked, fields throbbed with ripe tomatoes. Farmers couldn't give them away. A perfect, beautiful tomato crop rotted in the field. Many consumers, instead of educating themselves about salmonella and bathing tomatoes in a vinegar and water bath prior to consumption, opted to do without that southern summertime specialty. Even worse, the salmonella disaster cost Georgia farmers an estimated $13.9 million dollars. However, the real tragedy wasn't discovered until the end of the season when the CDC determined that peppers from Mexico, not Georgia-grown tomatoes, were making people sick.

Hopefully, Virginia, a valuable lesson was learned. Wash vegetables before consumption.

While I preferred my tomato sandwich with bacon and a slice of cheese, Billy liked his adorned with a fried egg. Around twelve o'clock each day we took a break from the garden. Billy allowed me to take over the kitchen. I'd fry two eggs in his cast iron skillet and toast a couple slices of bread while he sliced imperfect tomatoes that he refuses to sell to his "clientele." After he thanked the good Lord for our food and "all our many blessings," we would drink a large swig of iced tea and discuss the salmonella debacle. We wiped our mouths as juice ran down our chins. We dabbed dollops of mayonnaise that accumulated in the corner of our mouths and pitied those who were afraid of consuming what God had generously provided.

I believe the salmonella scare was, in part, one reason for Billy's business. That coupled with the trend to support local farmers and the sheer enjoyment people get when visiting his place. Billy Albertson is as real as they come. A trip to the farm is almost magical. It's like stepping back in time. One minute you're sitting in six lanes of traffic asking God why in the world you moved to Atlanta, the next a rooster crows a warning to stay away from his hens.

Even though Billy's farm is organic, his operation is not a pick your own or "U-pick" farm. In his words, he "can't turn every Tom, Dick, and Harry loose in the garden." Instead, as the sun awakens the rooster, and before the road starts humming with traffic, he buckles his overalls, slips bare feet into well-worn sneakers, and pushes a wheelbarrow into the field long before most folk roll out of bed.

Billy Albertson is seventy-seven-years-old. For the record, I am not. A southern lady never reveals her age. It seems these days, a southern lady spends Friday having her nails done before she leaves town to enjoy the weekend at her Jekyll Island beach house. She certainly doesn't callous her hands pushing a wheelbarrow, or break polished nails picking tomatoes.

By the way, I'm thirty-five years younger than Billy. In theory, I should be able to gather any vegetable twice as fast, or at least *as* fast as he does. I can't, even though I've tried many, many times.

The garden was thick with over one hundred Park's Whopper vines planted in four rows. Experience has taught me that early in the morning the rows seem short then mysteriously get longer the hotter the temperature. Around one o'clock, when it's ninety degrees in the shade, I'd swear that last row was five miles long.

Like most farmers, Billy has tried many ways to increase his crop. He knows what works best for his "tow-maters." He knows when to fertilize and when to water. While other farmers control insects with dust and spray, he applies chemicals only when absolutely necessary. He'd rather have a decreased harvest than use chemicals. As a result, tomatoes from his garden are smaller than those available in the grocery store. Some have worm holes in them, although he feeds those to the goats. Others sport small cracks near the stem, a result of moisture fluctuations in the soil. The tomatoes are imperfect, yet delicious.

My grandpa would say, "They are so good it makes your tongue slap your brains out."

Billy is a man of abundant wisdom, if I take the time to listen. He utters words that might not make sense at the time like, "watch out for packsaddles in the corn." He speaks in a cadence few understand, with a vernacular many would mock. His advice, or "isms" is always spoken for my benefit. More about those pesky packsaddles later. Right now there are tomatoes to pick.

There is a certain method to harvesting. All total Billy owns six metal wheelbarrows in a variety of sizes and structural integrity. Several have small holes rusted through the shell. Two don't have tires. They run on rust covered rims, the rubber long since removed once they stopped holding air. While many would throw away these dull and deteriorating tools, the holey wheelbarrows make harvesting easy.

Billy placed two empty five gallon buckets in each wheelbarrow and then headed out toward the field. I followed.

"Experience is the best lesson," is a phrase Billy uses often. While I would never argue with a man of such gumption, I prefer learning from others rather than suffer my own misgivings and painful inadequacies. For those who agree let me impart a tiny bit of personal experience.

9

Lesson one in wheelbarrow driving: Drive at your own pace. Look directly at the ground ahead of you. Do not attempt to catch Billy, whose long legs make two steps to your one. Ignore the tomato plants grabbing your sleeve begging, "Pick me . . . pick me, I'm ripe!" Don't be distracted by the goats begging for food. They are liars and will say anything for a vine-ripened tomato. I know this now only because I was running so hard to catch Billy that I missed the narrow wooden plank that serves as a bridge across the drainage ditch.

Yes, I crashed. I'm sure he saw me. If he didn't, there was no mistaking the clatter of buckets tumbling about. I righted myself and quickly tossed them back inside the wheelbarrow then pretended nothing had happened. How could he keep a straight face with all the clacking commotion I was making? I then had to run faster to try and catch up. The buckets bounced, making even more noise.

He laughed. I could tell.

I stood beside him, hands on hips, inhaling gulps of humid air.

"I like to pick here and work yon side toward the house," he said while pointing toward the garden. "That way when it gets hot, you don't have so far to push your load."

"Yon side" is the opposite of where you are currently standing.

I liked his approach. I adjusted my sun visor and reached for a tomato. And so began the first of many races.

Billy is about six feet tall. He stoops a bit, possibly out of habit, because he's used to harvesting from vines shorter than he. I'm five foot tall; in theory, I am the perfect "tow-mater" picker.

He placed an empty bucket in my hand and gave me instructions. "Just snap the tow-mater off the vine like this," he said while his hand reached inside the rusty tomato cage.

Snap. Like a magician, he grabbed a tomato, flicked his wrist and presented me with a perfect stem-less vegetable that was ready to wash and sell to the next available customer.

"Leave the stem on the vine," he instructed. "It scratches and pokes holes in the peeling."

I nodded. That made sense. This would be easy.

I'm not the most coordinated person, but each time I tried to snap a tomato off the vine, it refused to let go. While I tugged and vowed next time to bring my scissors, Billy emptied his bucket into the wheelbarrow twice before I finished harvesting the first plant. Gathering "Tommy Toes" what some folk call "Cherry Tomatoes," was my niche. I could wedge my hands between the spaces in the cages and with nimble fingers have a basket full in no time.

Once the wheelbarrows were piled high, we pushed them-one of us slower than the other-to an outdoor sink. A garden hose was clamped to the corner of a bathroom sink. Billy received the sink from a friend who was renovating a bathroom. He efficiently converted unwanted trash into a useful tool he uses daily. Billy unclamped the hose and rolled the wheelbarrow to the edge of a smaller vegetable garden with cucumbers trellised six feet high. This is when the holey wheelbarrow came in handy. Rinse water drained into the smaller garden where green beans were planted. Billy removed a cloth towel from his back pocket and tossed it to me. Turning, he pointed his burden to a table located in the carport.

"You dry while I sack." He instructed.

I dried quickly and gently laid the tomatoes on the table.

Billy grabbed a variety of different sized tomatoes, placed them in a plastic bag, and weighed them on a scale that's probably sixty years old. "Some folk want to buy only large tow-maters, some want only small ones. I mix and match 'em, that way everyone's happy," he said.

I worked quickly while watching him from the corner of my eye. He wasted no time, grading the culls into a pile that would be delivered to charity when time allowed. He held each bag for a split second as if calculating the weight in his hand, then laid the bag on the scale.

"Always better to err on the side of weighing too much than too little," he said while plucking tomatoes from the table at a pace I couldn't match.

Billy's customers always get more than they pay for.

Moisture accumulated on the towel as I struggled to keep up. Soon, the table was filled with a pre-weighed bagged, and ready-to-go bounty.

"I think it's time to put out the sign and get some customers in here," Billy finally said.

I took a seat and welcomed the break.

He loped toward the end of the drive carrying a white hand-painted "tomatoes" sign with black lettering. Three cars turn into the driveway before he returned. My chest tightened. I'd never seen anything like it. I thought it would be hours, not seconds, before the first customer arrived. Obviously they knew something about Billy's vegetables that I didn't.

11

"Here," he said while handing me a small cherry tomato. "It looks like you could use a snack. Pop this in your mouth and tell me what you think."

Cherry tomatoes are my least favorite. Small and filled with seeds I've always found them bitter and unappealing. I rolled it between my fingers, then popped it in my mouth. Billy waited for my response. The tart, yet sweet globe spewed rich juice inside my mouth.

"Wow. I've never tasted anything like this," I said sincerely.

He nodded. "Goat manure makes the best tasting tomatoes," he offered with a smile.

Chapter Three

Jealousy, It's Not Just For Children

"These children do not have proper upbringing."
—Renea Winchester

The farm hummed with new life renewing my spirit after a lethargic winter. Baby chicks had just hatched, which filled the farm with peeping furry critters. Naturally, my daughter wanted all her friends to see the newest arrivals on the farm. After all, where else can one find baby goats and chicks in a busy metropolitan city?

Billy placed a newly hatched chick in Jamie's hand and said, "Ain't nothing quite like the sound of a baby chick chirping next to your ear."

Instinctively, she cocked her head and placed it to her ear, then smiled. Jamie let her friend hold the peeping creature, but became a bit bossy when her friend wouldn't give it back. Billy nodded and smiled knowingly.

During the excitement of the moment, the girls failed to latch the chicken coop. Soon, the prized rooster was loose. He strutted—his red comb bobbing in defiance—as he swaggered across the lawn. With feathers fluffed he dared us to catch him. We immediately established a four point perimeter and walked, arms outstretched, toward the escapee in an attempt to encourage him back inside the coop. The rooster, recognizing his freedom, ducked his head and bolted for the woods.

It's amazing how fast a rooster can run.

"Try to cut him off before he gets to the neighbor's house," Billy said while making his way toward the rooster.

I tried to close in on the escapee, but he flew to the top of the woodshed and crowed.

"That's alright," Billy said. "Once he settles down, I'll capture him."

The next day I asked Billy if he'd had caught the wayward rooster.

"Oh no," he said while pointing to a pile of feathers, "but the hawk did."

I was crushed. I started crying. The rooster would have still been alive had we not visited.

Billy continued, "I came out this morning and feathers were everywhere. The hawk must have got him this morning when he tried to get back inside with the hens."

The thought of the poor rooster being killed as the hens watched broke my heart. One careless mistake and he was dead.

Billy pulled me into his arms and squeezed. "Now don't worry. I reckon that old hawk was hungry. They got to eat too ya know."

That didn't help me feel better.

I had started telling Mother about my adventures at Billy's hoping to keep her spirits high and her mind off the weeks of chemotherapy lurking ahead. I shared the rooster debacle, relaying my guilt while blowing my nose and gulping for air.

"It's our fault," I said with a hiccup. "We're supposed to be helping Billy with his work, but because of us the rooster died."

Mother offered sage advice that did nothing to ease my pain. "Death is a part of life," she said.

I like this advice about as much as the familiar "death and taxes" statement. I withheld my opinion as she continued.

"When I was twelve-years-old, Daddy brought a little filly home for me. I was thrilled. I'd read *Black Beauty* and *National Velvet* so many times the edges of the books were threadbare. I dreamed of owning a horse of my own, but we only had Prince, the work horse."

I captured each word and locked them in my heart. Stories about her father, who died before I was born, were few.

Mother continued, "I named her Lightning because she had a white blaze down her forehead. Daddy agreed to care for her during the day while I was at school if I'd be responsible for her in the morning and afternoon. Not once did he need to remind me to take care of her. Soon, she was old enough to join Prince in the field. I let her out one morning, and when I called for her that afternoon she didn't come. We found her at the top of the mountain. She had stepped into a bee's nest. We guessed she was kicking at the bees or trying to scratch as they stung and somehow her hoof got caught in the halter. Her neck was broken."

Mother paused. I could almost see her wiping away tears. "I guess I'm saying that I know what it feels like to lose an animal."

"But Mom, I still feel responsible," I said.

"Of course you do. But you must remember, if you've got it to love, you've got it to lose."

"Thanks, but that doesn't make me feel any better," I said.

"It didn't help me at the time either, but it's still the truth. If you're going to share you heart with any living thing at some point you're going to have some pain," she offered.

I knew she wasn't referring to the rooster, or her horse.

Sharing is a problem all children have. Most don't want to share their toys, or in this case farm animals. As adults we are supposed to recognize jealous characteristics and avoid them. But as other helpers entered Billy's garden, jealousy plucked at my spirit. I, like my daughter, had begun to feel that a small portion of his farm was mine. I didn't want to share Billy.

My protective tendency increased after an incident with the baby goats. I lack the ability to understand what possessed a mother (other than complete ignorance) to allow her small children unsupervised access to the goats. This particular parent, whom I shall call Abigail, opened the gate and turned her two small boys inside the pasture. She latched it behind them and watched safely from the other side as they gave chase. In an attempt to protect their kids, the nannies cried out and ran toward the safety of the barn. Excited by this, the boys chased even harder. I'm no expert, but even I could tell that the nannies were frightened. Abigail stood outside the fence casually chatting with Billy who kept one eye on her and the other on her terrorizing twosome.

I know it sounds judgmental, but I thought, *if someone gets hurt she'd be the type to sue.* That happens all the time. Parents turn their children loose to "be children." They offer no supervision or boundaries as their offspring runs wild and exhibits destructive behavior. These are the same mothers who coo at their children and call them, "Precious, Princess, Darling and Dear." They don't believe in discipline but believe in raising unencumbered "free spirits." Then when little Johnny, I mean little "Precious," falls in an uneven pasture and scrapes his knee, or gets bee stung after stirring up a nest (something no homeowner can prevent), Mom's suing to take everything Billy's got.

I watched in shock as both boys scaled the chain link fence, then dropped into the section where the male goats, the ones with horns, are kept.

Abigail showed no concern.

At this point Billy excused himself and entered the pasture. He isn't the type who would call someone else's child down, unlike myself who was about to shout, "Get your wild asses off the fence before I come in there and jerk a knot in your tail."

Of course, the knot jerking should begin with the mother. I mean really, who does she think she is? No, seriously, at what point does anyone bring their children to someone else's property and watch them terrorize defenseless animals? After all, Billy's pasture isn't a petting zoo. But the boys weren't finished. Once they grew tired of the goats, they stomped through the vegetables, ruining crops in the process, and then started climbing trees.

Abigail said nothing. Billy said nothing. I was about to scream, but I said . . . nothing. I kept quiet because I didn't want Billy angry with me. I understand why Abigail didn't correct the boys. In her eyes, her perfect children were doing nothing wrong. Part of me expected Billy to call the children down, but he probably felt it wasn't his place to discipline them.

My parents taught me that character is how one acts when no one is looking, and here both boys were tearing the place down while everyone watched. I wonder how Abigail would feel if I invited myself into her home then proceeded to walk all over her couch with my manure-laden shoes? Oh, the thought of it made me smile. While her little darlings dangled from tree limbs, I envisioned my footprints on Italian marble leading into the living room.

Trust me, my shoes are manure-laden.

Just because we were on a farm didn't mean Billy's things were any less valuable than hers. I believe that character is shown wherever one goes, and while my character reveals I'd like to shake some sense into her bubble-head and walk on her couch with stinky shoes; she exhibited complete disrespect for Billy's property. What's worse, she encouraged her children's behavior by not explaining the value of his property. Obviously no one had taught her how to treat others the same way she wanted to be treated.

Of course just yesterday the rooster had died because of us, but that was an accident. I constantly remind Jamie to treat Billy's things with respect. I had explained the importance of closing all doors and gates.

16

When I spoke with Mother she and I vowed I'd find a replacement rooster in North Carolina and deliver it to him after my next visit with her.

As Abigail loaded her brood into her vehicle I marveled at Billy's patience. Honestly, I don't know how he held his tongue. Never one to say anything unkind, he thanked them for coming, then after they left we did our best to repair the damage they'd left behind.

Visitors to Billy's farm are often assigned "chores." He can always find something for folk to do regardless of age or ability, that is if they're willing to get their hands dirty and sweat a little. However, most people prefer to "visit" instead of "help," that is until they need something.

It's remarkable how many friends Billy suddenly obtains when okra and tomatoes become ripe. It's the same phenomenon many homeowners experience after installing a swimming pool in the backyard. Overnight, the field ripened and the farm hummed with helpers. People drove from the North Georgia Mountains to "help" pick tomatoes. They arrived around one o'clock, conveniently after most of the crops had been harvested.

I thought, *where have they been all summer?* as I watched them tumble from the car. Surely it was obvious that these so called helpers had ulterior motives. I'm not implying they came solely for free vegetables, nor am I saying that I never took vegetables home. I did. Each time I offered to pay like everyone else. Billy always refused.

"You don't know how much help you've been to me," he'd say while grabbing a plastic bag. "Here, sack up some tow-maters and carry them home with you."

I'd bag up the culled tomatoes with bug holes and split tops; things he'd never sell. Then, while Jamie distracted him, I'd slip money into the barrel. I hope the other helpers did the same.

Chapter Four

Charity, Religion, and Goat Manure

"It's the job of the church to care for the poor."
—Billy Albertson

Many have heard the expression, "he'd give you the shirt off his back." Those words ring true for Billy Albertson. When summer heat blistered my shoulders, he produced a thin long-sleeved cotton shirt and insisted I wear it into the field. Even though I carried my own water to the farm, he made sure I kept hydrated and insisted I drink every drop of Gatorade he offered.

I complied, even though I detest the taste of Gatorade.

It's hard to imagine a farm with less than three acres of property, almost half of which is goat pasture, producing enough fresh vegetables to sell to the public. I had no way of measuring how many bushels of beans, squash, cucumbers, and tomatoes we picked. I only knew that I worked each morning from eight until after lunchtime. It seemed the more I picked, the more there was to harvest.

Each time I helped Billy he offered to pay me. When I declined he'd push money toward me and say, "You don't know how much you've hoped me."

"Hoped" is old-timers speak for the word help, not that he's old.

He'd grab vegetables and sneak them into my car as payment. My help created an uncomfortable situation that left him feeling indebted and me embarrassed accepting his generosity. I helped because of the pleasure I got out of the arrangement. I needed to keep my hands busy. As long as I worked until I was exhausted, I hadn't the energy to worry about Mother. Trust me, when my worry and stress became unmanageable I would have paid to work in Billy's garden. Still, he doesn't like to be beholden, (meaning indebted) to anyone. He always gives more than he receives. We're twins in that regard. So when I refused his method of payment, I hurt his feelings. Eventually, I proposed a workable solution. I'd work for goat manure.

Early in the spring, before my daffodils erupted, I had developed an elaborate plan. I'd clear off a spot below my house for a vegetable garden. For weeks I moved rocks, trimmed brush, and dug up roots preparing my fantasy garden plot. My garden would be spectacular, I imagined. I'd have tomatoes the size of dinner plates, salads made with fresh lettuce, and onions grown with my own two hands. I would be the Martha Stewart of the neighborhood. I believed it until I dumped the first shovel of dirt into the wheelbarrow.

Growing vegetables at my place wouldn't be easy. I was cursed was infamous Georgia clay, a slippery mess when wet and cement-hard when dry. I would need mounds of organic matter incorporated into the soil before I'd have an area suitable for planting. I explained my plan to Billy, complete with a job-site field trip. He agreed. I was in desperate need of the best fertilizer on the market, goat manure. Now instead of trying to out-give each other, we reached an arrangement. He had something I needed and I'd pay for it with manual labor. We were both pleased.

"I reckon I'd help anybody who needs it," he once told me while leaning back in a seat he called the "captain's chair" which was a lopsided aluminum lawn chair with green and white threadbare plastic weaving.

"But they've got to be making an effort," he continued. "I figure if everyone was doing their part we'd jump right in and help someone in need. That way the gov-mint wouldn't need to get involved."

I thought about that while he continued.

Billy's eyes sparkled as he said, "The Bible uses the word slothful. I believe you should earn your living by the sweat of your brow. That's what the Bible says, but these days most people don't earn a living that way. I like to work. I'm always going, doing . . . always on the move."

That's an understatement. I practically have to duct tape the man to his captain's chair to keep him still.

As comfortable as Billy is in the garden, he does, on occasion leave the farm. Some might find it hard to believe that this simple man holds a passport and has done quite a bit of traveling. During a trip to Holland with his daughter, Janet, he asked one of the locals, "Who takes care of the poor?"

The local's response: "It's the church's job to take care of the poor."

I thought to myself, *how many people have taken vacations outside of the country? At any moment were they concerned about the poor? Did they ask the natives who takes care of the less fortunate?* I'm ashamed to say that I haven't.

Billy paused for a moment. His blue eyes twinkled with mischief as he relayed the story. "I believe that we are the church. So Zippy, answer me this question, why don't we help each other out?"

For a goat farmer he asks profound questions.

Billy's daughters wanted to show him the world, but his wife's illness and farm obligations hindered their dream. Janet told me that for a while she was sad but, "God provided him with wonderful cultural experiences in his own backyard. Over the years people from all over the world have stopped by his house. When Daddy says, 'You're not from around here, are you?' it gives visitors an opportunity to tell him where they are from. Daddy just loves people so they feel comfortable telling him their views on politics, religion and the way they lived in their home country. They have brought him gifts and food from all over the world," Janet said.

"Different cultures like different things from the farm. The people from Jerusalem who he calls the "Israelites" love the figs. People from Kenya, Mexico and Jamaica love the goats and chickens; and the people from Asia love all the vegetables. What tickles me is that they come and enjoy his little farm and say 'this place is *just* like Kenya,' or, 'this place is *just* like Mexico,' or, 'this place is *just* like my village in Asia.' In a way Daddy is getting to see the world just like I had wished for him without stepping off his property," she concluded.

Billy believes the Bible is God's holy word. He once told me, "If you read the Bible it tells you how to live. It even tells you how to vote. Take the ten commandments and apply them to anyone who's running for office and you'll know right then who to vote for regardless of their political party."

As I said, pretty deep thinking for a goat farmer.

Billy attends a church so small that it only has services twice a month. He's invited me to visit saying, "We ain't got no fancy choir, and our preacher ain't appointed by someone wearing a robe. Our preacher is called by God. All we got to offer folk is the gospel."

I have to say that's a refreshing theology. Today many are too busy to attend church. I've heard people say, "I don't have to be in church to be near God or to experience the Holy Spirit." I won't argue that point for a second. We can hold church at a traffic light or on the basketball court. Anytime we reach out to God, He's there. However, going to church is one of the few times I can publicly show others that I care enough about my Savior to give Him my time.

Many churches are now holding "contemporary services" in an effort to attract a younger, less formal and more diverse congregation. That's fine for some, but I still wear what Mother calls my, "Sunday best" clothes. Wearing jeans into a Sunday service isn't the best I have to offer.

I'm not sure if Billy knows how much church is held in his garden. I personally have had several conversations with God while picking vegetables on my knees. Billy once shared a story about a visitor who asked for permission to go off into the field and pray.

"I told him, 'why of course. You pray anywhere you feel comfortable,'" Billy said.

I imagine it was an honor to have someone pray in his garden. Kind of like having his own personal mission field in the backyard.

Billy firmly believes in loving his neighbor and everyone he meets falls into the "neighbor" category. The next door neighbor, Mark, plants a garden adjacent to Billy's. The property line mingles so close only they can tell what crop belongs to whom. Mark's gardening style is advanced. Billy calls it, "high-tech," with "state-of-the-art watering hoses and fancy staked plants." Mark owns a tractor, that's painted. The paint wore off Billy's tractor before I was born. Billy waters the vegetables using a dented tin cup. Tomatoes are staked using rusty cages that are tied with recycled orange rope. Theirs is a friendship based on respect, admiration, and perhaps a touch of friendly competition thrown in, just for fun.

Billy's neighbors extend beyond the property boundary. He knows a couple of folk who are "deprived of driving privileges," meaning their health, or eyesight, has deteriorated to the point that they no longer drive. Using Billy's words, he "carries" these people to lunch, to the cemetery to visit graves of loved ones, and to appointments. He never expects payment. After all, payment of any kind would be the ultimate insult. Who wants to be paid for doing what God commands?

Billy has "carried" me a time or two. I'll never forget one particular trip. We were picking up something in his truck. I'd told him my vehicle would haul the load, but he insisted on driving so we piled into his old white truck. The windshield wipers-frozen mid-swarp- obstructed my view of the road. With the trucked loaded, Billy cranked the truck and eased it into first gear. Or at least he tried. He pulled the gearshift, shook his head slightly and said two words I didn't want to hear, "Aw man."

I turned toward him, but before I could ask what was wrong he bent forward and began rummaging through a pile of tools tucked under the seat. I heard implements clanging against each other and leaned over to get a look. He emerged with a tiny hammer. Oh it was the cutest thing I had ever seen. It was a tiny little tool with two metal heads.

I'd never seen a two-headed hammer before. Where I'm from a claw hammer gets the job done.

"Don't worry. She's done this before," he said then hopped out of the truck and disappeared. Before I could register what he was about to do, the sound of metal hitting metal reverberated beneath the floorboard.

There must be a legion of angels assigned to watch over Billy. My first thought was, *The truck is going to run over him.* My second thought was, *I'm going to have to call his daughters and tell them he's been run over, and then they're going to kill me.*

While he pounded away at the underside of the truck, I prayed for his safety and thought, *Please let him fix this and not get hurt because they'll never believe me if I have to explain.*

"The steering column's stuck again," I heard above the clatter. "Just sit tight. In a minute you'll see the gearshift move," he promised.

At this point I began working my way toward the steering wheel, left foot first. I reasoned my toe might reach the brake pedal moments before the truck started rolling.

Ping. Ping. Ping.

I inched closer. With one hand on the steering wheel, and my foot on the brake, I watched as the metal lever jiggled slightly. A pop sounded and the lever moved.

"There she goes," he confirmed.

With agility I could never match, he reappeared from beneath the truck while I tried to return to my place on the passenger side and pretend like he hadn't just scared one full year off my life.

As he entered the truck, I reached for the hammer, hoping he wouldn't notice my hand shaking. "What kind of tool you got there?" I asked.

"Oh that there's a ball peen hammer," he answered. "I keep it in case of emergencies. I bought this here truck forty years ago. My girls keep saying I need a new one, but as long as she's running, she'll be fine."

I wasn't going to argue with his logic.

From the looks of it, there had been an abundance of emergencies. The handle was worn smooth. Layers of sweat and oil had turned the handle a dark brown color, while both heads of the hammer were shiny from use.

Billy shifted the truck into gear and "carried" me safely home.

Chapter Five

Paddling in School and Parenting Today

"I'd like to talk to the man who decided paddling is wrong."
—Billy Albertson

"Kids these days need boundaries," Billy has told me many times. "Right now, they're ruling the roost and their parents let 'em."

It's no secret that being a parent is one of the hardest jobs in the world. Children are under tremendous pressure, but so are parents. Children are inundated with unrealistic images through every media avenue. In the days before Photoshop, teen idols used makeup to cover unsightly imperfections. Today, computer programs manipulate images which are then marketed toward our youth who have a false impression of reality. Any magazine is an example.

"When I was in school," Billy said, "if you misbehaved the teacher gave you a paddlin'. Then when you got home, your parents gave you another one."

I myself have been paddled in school, but I wasn't going to tell Billy. My crime: passing notes. I was writing bad things about the teacher's pet. I flexed my creative writing muscle at an early age and my first critic, Mrs. Lindsey, didn't appreciate my style. After the paddling I never passed another note in class . . . ever.

Today, instead of passing notes people text. It seems that children, and adults alike, can't walk and talk without their fingers on a button. According to my daughter, she's the only one in the universe who doesn't have texting. I also veto MySpace, Twitter, instant messaging and whatever else society has in store to lure her into the cesspools available today. While my life isn't as simple as Billy's, I do try to keep distractions to a minimum.

Still, my daughter is under an exceptional amount of pressure to text. We've all seen the kids sitting next to each other fingers moving rapidly across the buttons of their phone. They are texting each other when all they have to do is turn their heads and speak. At this point in the "instant world" we live in, no texting privileges could mean having no friends. At age twelve, she's "the only person in school" who doesn't have text and email options on her phone. While I doubt this is true, she asks multiple times each day for texting capabilities and each time receives a firm, "no" for an answer. Saying "no" is all about control.

She pouts. She screams, "You hate me. I hate my life. I don't ever get anything I want." These tantrums, while painful for us both, do not change my mind. I must hold firm to the boundary I have established in order to raise a daughter with character.

As a mother, it is my job to limit the avenue pedophiles, murderers, bullies, and other individuals have. And as long as I say no, I limit that access. I may shock the world when I say, "It is *my* responsibility to raise my daughter. Not the church, the school, and certainly not her peers." I'm the parent and no amount of pressure will sway me. So, bring on the tantrums, the texting stops here.

I am also against texting after what occurred on the last day of school when I hosted an end of the year dance party for six girls. I naively assumed each guest came to have fun. One particular girl spent the entire time texting her "boyfriend." Not only that, but at one point I noticed all the guests were outside. I found them huddled around this child, and I do use the word *child* accurately, listening to her talk on her cell. She had placed the phone on speaker and was showing them an example of how to talk to boys. The girls huddled around her, captivated by the ease with which she spoke and her demanding attitude.

Of course, Billy doesn't have a cellphone, but he does have numerous friends and offers sage advice on friendships. "To have a friend, you've got to be a friend," is something Billy told his children while they were growing up. I shared his words with Jamie hoping to teach her how to act at parties.

"Patty's behavior was disrespectful," I explained to Jamie whose arms were crossed in that *I'm not listening*, stance. "Even when your friends told her it was time to put her phone away and join the party she ignored them. It looks like she used your party as an excuse to spend time talking to her boyfriend."

26

A crease appeared on Jamie's forehead. I prayed some of my words were sinking in; it's hard to tell.

"She wasn't acting like she wanted to be your friend at all, now was she?" I asked.

The crease deepened.

"So Jamie, next time we host a party, I'll explain to the parents that I'll be collecting all cell phones at the door. That way nothing will interfere with guests having a good time," I continued.

That should go over well. What I didn't tell Jamie was I will also explain to the parents that someone used our last party as an excuse to text her boyfriend. Maybe other parents will agree with my decision, follow my lead and host their own text-free events. If not, at least I've sent the message that I have boundaries.

Young girls are bombarded with images of sexuality through various media avenues. Even worse, many parents encourage their girls to have real "boyfriends" in middle school. Unsupervised dating is also happening at an early age as are serious, exclusive relationships. In an effort to increase their child's popularity, some parents host boy-girl parties. Girls are draped in tight fighting shirts and low-rise jeans. As if the low-rise craze isn't enough, thong underwear is now available for girls as young as ten. At this point all I can do is shake my head and ask, "When did it become acceptable for pre-teen girls to wear thong underwear, padded bras and have physical relationships?" Equally important is the question, "Why aren't parents writing letters, boycotting manufacturers and saying no to this trend?"

I'm afraid the answer is convenience laced with a spirit of non-confrontation. As a parent, it's easy to say "yes" and painful to say "no." Especially when my daughter is correct, everyone else *is* doing it. Saying no is one of the most tedious parts of being a parent.

When I mentioned this to Billy he shook his head and said, "Girls always scared me to death. When I was growing up, I was afraid to talk to them."

Today, he'd be petrified. I know I am.

Billy's advice is to "do what your heart says." This doesn't mean allow emotions to take over and fulfill every physical need and urge. He is refer-ring to the seed of truth (your conscience if you will), planted deep inside the heart. He believes, and I agree, that each heart possesses a well of truth we can draw from when we need direction.

I have described this sensation to my daughter saying, "If the hair on the back of your neck is standing up and you feel a tingle creeping up your spine, that's your cue to stop for a moment and rethink your actions."

I think I'm the only parent in the universe offering this advice.

When I was a child, and let me pause to say that I do *not* consider myself old, respect for every elder wasn't just expected; it was demanded. Adults used to demand respect. After all they provided a roof over my head and hand-me-down clothes to cover my nakedness. Parents were working numerous hours to make their children's lives better. If there was an adult in the room, be it your parent or not, they were in charge. Adults had the authority to correct any child who was out of control. I don't mean beat the child, but I do mean call them aside, and discuss their actions and the consequences. Billy says with infinite wisdom, "When we stopped correcting children we started doing society wrong. How can we expect kids to do what's right if we don't teach them?"

Today, woven beneath the giggly undertone of situation comedy shows, parents are portrayed as stupid. Children talk back to their parents. They lie, steal, and worse. Parents have become impotent teachers unable to equip our future with the simple facts of life. So let me dive in and offer a glimpse of reality. Life isn't about playtime, shopping, makeup and video games. Rules apply to everyone, from simple traffic rules to more difficult life standards like, we *should* be nice to people, (especially to parents who *are* buying, at the very least, the food you eat).

I am trying to teach my children that the world will not give you a blank check just because you have a nice personality and great smelling hair. I tell them, "if you believe what you see on television and mimic that behavior more than likely you'll lose your job and have difficulty with relationships."

Billy agrees. "That thing right there," he says with a finger pointed to his television, "has rurnt many families. Folk ought to turn that thing off and stop letting their kids play video games. Parents should make kids go outside and play."

Despite my constant efforts to use what Jamie experiences as examples of how not to act, I noticed a hint of Disney rubbing off on her. She was mimicking what she watched on television: spouting sarcastic comments, sashaying around the house, rolling her eyes all while thinking this behavior was cute and acceptable; which is exactly why we removed the television from our home.

Yup, it's gone. We're an unplugged family.

It was the trace of tone in her "tween-age" voice that motivated the decision, combined with a family hike gone bad. An easy walk in the woods to experience God's country beneath a canopy of shade trees catapulted us into the land of the unplugged. These days physical exercise of any form is basically child abuse. Both of the children lagged behind huffing and puffing, murmuring and complaining. They didn't enjoy the beauty of the outside world, but preferred—like a barn soured horse—the inside coolness and television fantasy land. That afternoon I asked myself why I had given a piece of equipment so much power. The following morning, the television had to go.

One would have thought we had physically beaten the children. Their whines of shock and disbelief were quickly replaced with the familiar phrase, "This is so unfair." And it was unfair; our family had become crippled by the boob tube.

"When I grew up there weren't no television," Billy said when I told him we were unplugged.

"We played outside," he continued. "We'd get a worn out rim and roll it up and down the road, or play in the creek. Naw, we didn't have no television and I turned out alright."

I'll admit there was a twinge of panic the day the technician disconnected the powerful cable which connected our family to hours of unlimited noise and time-consuming worthless information. As the weeks passed the glorious sound of nothing was comforting. The brain draining influence and power the television had on my family was gone. Hallelujah! No more laughter in a can, applause on demand, or watching spoiled children traipsing around the set of a fictitious life wearing padded bras, hair extensions and demanding purses that cost more than most people make in a month.

Chapter Six

Beans, Beans the Magical Fruit

"You don't know how much help you've been."
—Billy Albertson

This morning, while most people were still snoring, I parked my car in Billy's gravel driveway. I wore a baseball cap, sweat stained tee shirt and well worn sneakers. Billy stepped out of his house wearing overalls and no shirt. I'll never understand how some farmers can work all day beneath the blazing sun and never get the first freckle, whereas I have to be slathered head-to-toe in sunscreen or I'm blistered in thirty minutes.

Billy greeted me with a smile and placed a now familiar faded yellow bucket in my hand. He pointed to a spot in the garden opposite the tomatoes and said, "Go out there to the row beside the squash and pick the beans on yon side."

Before I could leave, he snatched the bucket from my hand. "You do know how to pick beans . . . right?"

I stood tall and stuck out my chin. Here was my chance to prove that I knew something about gardening. "Yes sir," I said. "I've picked beans before."

I rattled off bean picking protocol. "Be careful and don't knock the blooms off the plant. Pick only the beans that are full. Leave the undeveloped pods on the vine. Don't pull up, step on, or accidentally crush the vines because if you do, they'll die."

Billy returned the bucket to me and pointed his antiquated wheelbarrow toward the tomatoes and said, "Aw, you know what you're doing. Get on out there and start pickin'."

"Do you want me to leave the yellow pods for seed?" I asked.

Billy glanced over his shoulder and smiled at my infinite bean wisdom. "Oh yeah."

My mom would be proud.

I may be ignorant when it comes to growing tomatoes, but I know how to pick beans. Each year my parents cultivate a large garden thick with rows of white half runner beans. I have spent many childhood Saturdays sitting around a dishpan piled high with ripe green pods. Mom would unfold a piece of newspaper, lay it in my lap, and then place a double handful of them on the newspaper. I would string and snap until the very thought of another bean made me want to scream.

The fruit of a half runner resembles the fingers of someone with rheumatoid arthritis. Inside, large bumpy beans lie hidden between a thick green hull. During the summer months, homes all over my native western North Carolina mountains hiss with the sound of pressure cookers running non stop. Women sweat and toil inside tiny kitchens devoid of air conditioning, their hands swollen and crimson from hours of picking, stringing, and breaking. Sterilized Mason jars sit on the counter, waiting the arrival of another run of blanched beans. The day passes while a spaceship-looking silver cooker, spurts and hisses, as its pressure regulator dances against the vent pipe.

During the canning season, children are banned from the danger zone. This is women's work passed down from generation to generation. Snacks are left outside the kitchen door, and curious children are kept at bay with the wag of a wooden spoon. Each woman can recall frightening stories about exploding pressure cookers filling the kitchen with scalding steam, turning beans and broken glass into dangerous missiles. As night falls the kitchen quiets, save for the sound of lids sealing with a loud pop. No one asks what's for dinner. The answer is clear.

For those who prefer to enjoy beans without the hulls, harvest is delayed until the pods turn yellow and dry on the vine. Beans are then shelled, placed on quilts and driven to and from work where they quickly dry beneath the back window of the car. Once the beans have completely dried they are stored in airtight containers. Most folk call this bean "shelly's." In the winter months shelly's are prepared much like dried pintos. The thick luscious bean makes a delicious addition to soup, or prepared with butter and black pepper.

For old-timers, or those interested in heritage vegetables, white half runners can be picked in the summer then broken and strung together with needle and thread. The strings are then hung on porch rafters or in the attic to dry. This method creates a wrinkled mountain delicacy called "leather britches." In Billy's day, before canning was commonplace, people stored or "put up" fruits and vegetables this way. Leather britches are prepared by boiling them in water seasoned with thick slices of fatback.

I felt a sense of pride knowing I had earned his trust. Billy can't just turn any farmer wanna-be into his garden. It only takes one haphazard harvester to ruin a season of hard work.

"Don't pick the peas," he cautioned above the sound of tomatoes snapping off the vine. "They're not ready just yet."

I headed toward the squash plants swinging my bucket. I had a spring in my step. With a confident skip I envisioned myself being the best bean picker in these parts. I passed the squash and stopped hard. I dropped the bucket and studied the garden. The plants on yon side of the squash looked identical to the non-yon side. I didn't know what kind of beans Billy had, but they weren't half runners.

Weary from the weight of heavy vines, rows of corn leaned to one side seeking strength from the sun. Instead of driving stakes for the beans to climb, he had planted the bean and corn seeds together, like farmers did decades ago. Beautiful flat, non-bumpy beans dangled from beneath the stalks. From the bottom of the stalks to the tippy tippy top there were green beans turning yellow; green beans turning white; green beans turning purple; and green beans turning, well . . . green. I didn't want to pick the wrong thing and destroy his hard work, and I didn't want to look like an ignoramus either. I walked the rows trying to identify different species by their leaves. Unfortunately, they all looked alike. I examined the plants and tested the fullness by gently squeezing a few pods. That didn't help either. Dejected, I abandoned my bucket and returned to the ultimate knower of all things bean.

"Uuh, Billy," I said with my shoulders slumped. I felt like a kindergartner who had just spilled her milk. "I hate to bother you, but I really can't tell which beans I should pick."

There it was. A crease in the corner of his eyes, and another smile that almost said, "Bless her heart, she don't know nothing, but at least she's trying."

33

I half-way expected him to lead me by the hand as we returned to the tilting corn. He ignored the green beans that were turning purple and those turning yellow. He explained my confusion was because the fruit I saw hanging wasn't beans, but peas, specifically, "Zipper peas and pink-eye-purple-hull."

I had no idea what he was talking about.

He gently gathered a handful of pink-eye-purple-hulls in his hand and said, "This here is in high demand. It's what Georgia folk call a delicacy. I got people calling for these already and they won't be ready for another month."

I nodded like I'd remember this important bit of pea trivia, silently glad I hadn't picked them by mistake. It would be a pity to be fired after my first harvesting attempt. Billy pointed me to the correct crop and I began. An hour later I was finished. My second mistake was thinking I had finished after filling the first container. No sir, I walked to the end of the row, half dragging my heavy burden, to discover Billy had placed two more buckets and a wheelbarrow there.

"I thought you might be needing a few more vessels to get the row picked clean," he said.

Three buckets later, I steered my load to the carport. Billy pointed to the outdoor sink and said, "I like to give them a light rinse. It's so hot out here they'll wilt if we don't give them a drink."

My tee shirt clung to my body and judging by the smell, I could have used a light rinse myself.

Beans aren't pre-bagged like tomatoes. He explained, "If you put them in a bag, they'll sour."

Instead, they are placed in a plastic bin and sold, according to him, by the "handful." There is often a waiting list for his vegetables. As I was placing the beans in the carport, he stopped me.

"Put one of those buckets inside the house," he said. "I've already called a customer to come pick those up."

I opened the door and set the container inside while keeping most of my body outside. I was sweaty and grungy. Itchy dirt lined the crook of my arm and rubbed the back of my neck raw. I planned on keeping my dirty self outside the house, but Billy had other plans. With today's crop picked, he invited me inside for a sandwich and something to drink. We left our shoes at the door, imprinting sweaty footprints on the linoleum as we entered the kitchen. I'd taken to bringing my own drink because, honestly, I don't like the taste of Gatorade. Billy had noticed. There was a gallon of sweet tea in the refrigerator.

"I was thinking about canning these here beans," he said while uncovering several plastic bowls of beans. "Do you know how?" he asked me.

I imagine that as a child, Billy was responsible for the growing and harvesting side of food preparation. I don't mean to sound sexist, but canning was women's work. I guess it was a good thing I knew my way around a pressure canner because there was a passel (meaning a vast quantity) of beans in the bowls. Immediately I began to panic. I couldn't recall the last time I'd put up beans without my mother's help, mainly because I'd *never* canned anything all by myself. I wasn't certain I could do it. Should I process the jars at ten pounds of pressure for fifteen minutes, or fifteen pounds of pressure for ten minutes? I couldn't remember, and the directions to the pressure canner, which was much older than I am, had long since vanished.

In my heart I wanted to do a good job. I always try to do my best. I didn't want to disappoint Billy or waste beans that would certainly spoil if they weren't properly canned. I had no choice but to use a lifeline. Since my mother was having a chemotherapy treatment, I had to call Grandma Wonderful.

I call her Grandma Wonderful because she is both my grandma and wonderful. Everything she bakes, especially cornbread, is delicious. She has long since stopped asking me where I am when I call her with silly questions, such as the one I was about to ask. Over the years I'd called asking a variety of questions like, "Tell me again how you make banana pudding;" and, "I'm in the mood for stew beef. I can't remember exactly how you make it. What do I need to do?" I often try replicating her recipes at friend's houses, without the benefit of a recipe, relying only on my failing memory and her to be there when I call.

One day I expect she'll answer the phone and say, "This is the umpteenth time I've told you I don't use eggs in my cornbread."

"Umpteenth" means a whole lot. Kind of like a "passel," only more. Grandma Wonderful uses the word "umpteenth" a whole lot with me.

She and Billy have both lost their spouses after more than fifty years of wedded bliss. Wouldn't it be nice if Cupid would unite these perfectly matched lonely people? Since both still wear their wedding rings, I doubt that will ever happen. Besides, I don't have time to play Cupid, I have beans to can.

"I'm canning beans," I said the moment Grandma Wonderful answered the phone. "I don't recall if it is ten pounds for fifteen minutes, or fifteen pounds for ten minutes, which is it?"

"Lord have mercy child, neither" she said. "It's ten pounds of pressure processed for twenty-five minutes. Anything less and you'll be food poisoned. And before you ask, no, I do not put an egg in my cornbread. I told you that last time."

Billy had done the hard part.

"I couldn't sleep last night," he said. "So I strung and broke these here beans. I figured I'd can them today before it got hot."

It was three o'clock in the afternoon. The kitchen had reached sweltering hours ago.

Billy retreated into the back of the house and returned with two box fans he placed in the hallway. Warm air circulated through the kitchen transforming the room into a convection oven. Empty jars were upside down on a towel, sterilized and ready to fill. He pulled a large stainless steel pot from beneath the stove and filled it with beans. He added water and turned on the stove. We watched them blanch a brilliant green hue.

"Now where did I put my canning funnel?" he asked.

With a clatter, he began rummaging through the drawers finding a wooden spoon which he handed to me. "Put this somewhere, we'll need it in a minute," he instructed.

There was no room to lay it down, so I held it while he continued the search and retrieve mission.

"Let me check my storage compartment," he said while opening the door to the built-in wall oven. "One of these days I'm going to clean this out."

Pots, pans, and a variety of other necessary kitchen items were hidden inside.

"I hid things in here from Marge when she was sick," he offered. "I've just not had the heart to clean it out."

The canning funnel resembled a metal tea cup, with a large opening instead of a solid bottom. He placed the aluminum funnel atop an empty jar and said, "All I remember about canning is that you always use a wooden spoon to stir with." He retrieved a teaspoon from the drawer then said, "Let's get started. You're in charge of the beans. I'll measure the salt."

I was excited to follow his instructions. This was an elusive part of the canning process I'd never experienced. My mother believed children somehow triggered canner explosions. Therefore, I'd always been relegated to bean-stringer and breaker. In this oven-of-a-kitchen, standing beside a man who six months ago was a complete stranger, I became what he and my mother would both consider a real woman. From garden to jar I now knew how to put up beans. I slid the loaded jars to Billy who sprinkled a teaspoon of salt into each one. We stood shoulder to shoulder, sweat mingling, fan humming noisily in the kitchen. Mother would be proud.

Today's activities had given me a story to share hopefully, one that would take her mind off the long road of treatments that lie ahead. Suddenly, a thought entered my mind stealing my breath. *What if God was getting ready to take my mother?* My eyes stung. *What if that is why Billy was in my life?* I closed my eyes. Mother's cancer is life-threatening. Everyday I carry the guilt of not being near her when she needs me, intermingled with family obligations that keep me in Atlanta. I've often wondered, is my mother going to die, and had God given me this place as a source of refuge and renewal?

My hands shook. I wanted to run outside and hide beneath the umbrella-like leaves of the squash. I wanted to fall on the earth and shout, "No. Please God. No, don't take her just yet. Give me more time to show her I've made something of my life."

A light touch on my elbow signaled that Billy was ready for another jar. I blinked back tears and focused on my task. Billy opened a box of can lids and returned to his wall-oven-storage-center where he retrieved a small stainless steel pot. He added enough water to cover the bottom, placed the lids in the water, and turned the stove on high. It was then I realized he'd tricked me. Only an experienced canner knows to preheat the lids before processing.

He placed the warm tops on the jars, secured them with shiny metal rings, and gently added them to the canner. I poured five cups of water inside. With a clank and a twist he closed the contraption, turned to me and asked, "What did Grandma Wonderful say?"

I laughed and said, "She said I was going to kill us both. We need to process them at ten pounds for twenty-five minutes."

Billy adjusted the temperature. Moments later, the air vent popped up. When the gauge registered fifteen pounds, steam spat from the vent pipe. He placed the pressure regulator (a metal cap that sits atop the canner and maintains pressure at the pound indicated) on top of the machine. Soon the rocking sound of the regulator dancing while beans processed mingled with the hum of the box fans.

Maybe next week we'll string leather britches.

Chapter Seven

Gathering Manure At The Coleman Manor

"I like to help the elderly."
—Billy Albertson

There was little Billy or I could do to ease the depression which came with the changing season. Soon, orange and yellow colored leaves would fall as the earth turned away from the sun. Even in the south where winters are mild, there can be months of dreary, drippy, depressing weather. There were no tow-maters to harvest. The seed beans and corn had been shelled and stored for spring planting. In short, we were bored.

Billy reminds me that "Idle hands are the devil's workshop."

I doubt he has to worry about the devil. Still, he and I always have a project. Today the project was manure gathering.

"I was just asslin' around this morning and thought today would be a good day to get a load of goat manure," he said before I could speak the word, "hello" into the telephone.

"Asslin'" means wasting time. Something we both despise.

He was waiting for me when I arrived. I tossed a pitchfork and shovel into the back of his truck while he threw two bottles of water and a pair of leather gloves with duct tape covering the thin places into the cab. Billy owns a 1969 Chevy pick-up similar to one my dad had when I was a child. Billy bought the truck new and, according to him, "she's been a good 'un." While this vehicle doesn't have one of those "fancy, modern day hemi engines," it serves him well.

He cleared a spot inside the cab by taking his arm and scraping everything on the seat into a pile between us. The floorboard was filled with staples all farmers need: rope, paper towels, gloves, and sundry tools. I placed my feet on the edge of the cab, climbed in, and tugged the heavy door closed, then searched for a place to put my feet. While I hunted for a seat belt, Billy pumped the gas pedal.

"Now what we're gonna hafta do here in order to get her to crank is say the magic words," Billy said as he placed one hand on the key, the other on the steering wheel. "Hocus pocus."

He looked at me and waited.

"Hocus pocus," I repeated.

Billy turned the key. She cranked the first lick.

"Be careful where you put your feet," Billy warned. "I saw a snake in here the other day."

I glanced at my shoes that had disappeared beneath a rope coiled in the floorboard. Slowly I brought my knees up and rested my feet against the dash. Though highly improbable, the thought of anything crawling up my pants leg is one of my biggest fears.

We reached the first traffic light when Billy said, "It's prolley safe to put your feet down now." A grin lined his face. "Cause I didn't see no snake."

The temperature was a glorious seventy degrees. A light wind blew puffy clouds across a perfect robin's egg blue sky. One couldn't ask for better fall weather on this manure gathering field trip. Billy turned on the air conditioning, meaning he rolled down the "wind-er" and stuck out his arm. Like a copycat, I did the same.

"I got the best air conditioning money can buy," he said as the truck came to a stop at the traffic light on the corner of King and Hardscrabble.

Billy had to constantly "give her a little gas," in order to prevent the truck from stalling. "Folk keep telling me I need a new truck," he said while maintaining steady pressure on the pedal with the tip of his boot. "I tell them 'naw, I just need to adjust the choke.' That's all she needs."

Driving this truck was a physical chore. People with small feet, like my size five and a half's, don't have a prayer driving this truck. Billy's left foot stomped the clutch making a dull thudding sound as his hand moved the gear shift. His right foot worked double-time; his heel pressed the brake pedal while his toe tapped the gas, feeding the truck just enough to keep her from stalling. When the light turned green, Billy popped everything into place with one smooth motion and we continued.

My hair whipped around, lashing my face and sticking in the corners of my mouth. There was something relaxing about riding down busy

Highway 92 with Billy that made me yearn for the good old days. People were friendly back then. They hung their arms out the window and tossed up a hand in friendly greeting to every passerby. Today, people travel with the windows up and the doors locked. Many have already forgotten their manners when behind the wheel. The glory days of the American automobile have passed. I imagine that one day no one will remember when trucks were made of steel instead of rubber and plastic.

When Billy was growing up, a man's word was his bond. Goats, chickens, cattle, and horses served as legal tender, as did home-grown vegetables. Even though folk didn't live as long as they do now, the slower paced lifestyle seemed better than the hectic demands of today's society. While I enjoy the convenience of buying groceries without traveling an hour, the volume of traffic in this chaotic, noisy world has a negative impact on me.

I've often thought I was born in the wrong decade. Technology, progress, and the hustle of city life are exciting but also overrated, noisy, and used without regard to others. I reached this conclusion the first time a cell phone rang in church and the lady excused herself to answer the call.

"I've got to take this call . . . it's important," she explained while leaving the pew.

"No problem. God will wait," the minister responded.

For me, that was the line. If we can't give God forty-five minutes of our time once a week, something's wrong.

I feel like I'm rushing around trying to do more than ever, exhausting myself and feeling less satisfied than when I started. It seems that many days there is no time for family, friends, self, and certainly not God. I personally can't remember the last time I sat still and did nothing. And I wonder why I'm stressed.

"Now this here place we're going to is going to make my place look fancy," Billy said jolting me back to the present. "I promise, you've never see-d anything quite like this before."

Without warning, he made a sharp left, bracing me with his arm to prevent me from crashing through the window. The truck came to a sudden stop. The rear bumper touched the white line of the state highway. The front kissed a metal fence adorned with a sign which read, "Please keep gate closed." Billy slipped the truck into neutral, stepped on the parking brake, and opened the door. The Chevy sputtered and hiccuped, threatening to give up her last gasp as he pushed the gate open. He returned to the truck, gave her some gas and drove through. Before he could argue, I jumped out and closed the gate behind us.

"Make sure you latch it back good," he called above the clattering pistons.

I waved an acknowledgment and then secured the chain by looping it around a rusty nail. One strong push and the rickety fence would collapse. I scurried like a rabbit through knee-high grass, hoping to avoid who knows what kind of scaly creatures. I scrambled inside the truck and Billy urged it along a dirt road.

The word road is a generous description. We traveled a glorified pig trail. Grass, tall enough to bale into hay, slapped the belly of the truck, jamming seeds into the cracks of the door. A canopy of trees shaded the ground transforming the noonday sun to shade. I craned my neck heavenward and saw dozens of decade-old trees. Billy pulled me toward him moments before a huge limb reached inside the cab of the truck.

"It almost got ya," he said while wearing the smile I'd grown to love.

As we climbed a small hill, green walnut husks ruptured beneath the tires with a loud "whoosh." I remembered the sound from my childhood. While waiting for the school bus, my brother and I would see who could roll the most walnuts into a recessed place of the driveway. The winner was the one who accumulated the most nuts with the least amount of stain on their sneakers. Sometimes we'd hide behind the trees and watch Dad run over the walnuts as he came home from work. We'd don his leather gloves and pick them up with care. A careless collector wore stains on their fingers for a week.

Ahead, the exquisite remnants of a neglected home place emerged from the grass. Two hedge bushes in need of trimming reached across a sagging front porch. Paint, if there had ever been any, had long since peeled away from the wooden clapboard siding. Piles of unopened shingles were stacked neatly at the corner of the house. I daresay any roofer who attempted to nail down a shingle would find himself falling through the rafters.

The house was unoccupied, dark, and lonely. Instantly curious, I wanted to peek inside the naked windows, roam the property, and explore the grounds for heritage flowers and shrubs. Empty houses cry out to me, begging me to enter. My parents taught me well. I know prowling through other people's things is wrong, but as I looked at this pale, sad, home something pulled me toward it. Memories were hidden inside beckoning, teasing me with the promise of excitement, offering a glimpse of history that could vanish forever.

There is an urgency deep inside me that longs to touch the way of life that used to be, and maybe, if I slow down long enough to listen, hear what the spirits from the past have to say.

"Billy, who lived in that house?" I asked already picturing myself, hands cupped around my face, peering inside the windows.

"Oh that's where Mr. Coleman lives. Now hang on, this here's goin' to take some maneuvering." He said while turning the steering wheel.

Before I could brace myself, the truck was bouncing backward, up hill, and getting dangerously close to a large walnut tree. As the space between truck and tree narrowed I believed at any moment I'd hear the sound of metal crunching against hardwood.

Not only was Mr. Coleman's property home for hard-to-find walnut trees, but exotic fig and lemon trees were scattered throughout. Dark nooks and deep crannies dotted the property providing excellent homes for every species of slithering varmint. If I were a snake this would be heaven. Scorpions probably lived in the places too dark for snakes, and it goes without saying that lizards were running about willy-nilly. And it might have been my imagination, but as the truck slowed beside a rick of cord-wood I could have sworn something moved outside my window.

Who knew what lurked on yon side of the goats? I'd never know because I wasn't leaving the comfort and safety of the truck until we were parked at the manure pile. I propped my feet up on the dashboard and folded my arms across my lap. Nope. I wasn't budging, not one inch.

"Zippy, I need you to hop out and tend the gate while I back her up to the goat house."

Of course there would be another gate. Mr. Coleman's property was locked up tight. What kind of thief would risk life, limb, and certain snakebite, to sneak in and steal . . . steal what . . . goats? Only a fool would trespass as I suspected that anyone who gates land filled with hedge bushes, critters, and overgrown weeds might also posses a shotgun and the skills to use it.

The moment my feet touched the grass I was surrounded by a pack of mixed-breed dogs. Billy held out his hand in the gesture one uses to command dogs to stay, except he was speaking to me.

"Just hold tight. I'll tell Mr. Coleman we're here," he instructed.

I obeyed and held my breath as they circled my ankles and growled. Billy stepped onto a side porch filled with items most people call junk. There were tires, plastic containers, a washing machine, and a tower of black plastic bags filled with what I can only guess was garbage. The men spoke for a moment as I peered around the back of the truck. Thousands of neatly stacked brick wrapped around the back of the house. It looked like the only thing Mr. Coleman needed to embark on a massive home repair project was a worker.

The sound of toenails tapping against plastic caused me to bolt for the truck. *Rats . . . Lord have mercy, it had to be rats,* I thought. I was reaching for the truck door when I heard a meow. I turned to see several small cats scampering across the bags. You've got to have ferocious felines in a place as overgrown as this or the rats would carry you away.

Billy stepped onto the porch with a small man dressed in slacks cinched tight above his navel with a thin black belt. Mr. Coleman wore a well-loved Peterbilt cap and thick black glasses I suspected were an original prescription from the early 1950s. He uttered, "God yeah," in response to everything we said. Billy addressed him as Mr. Coleman, a symbol of respect for his elder. I imagine it was difficult for Billy hearing God's name used in vain twelve times in three minutes, which is why he opted to get to work versus burning daylight chit chatting.

I held the last gate open as the truck punched backward even further into the woods stopping only when Billy reached a stretch of rickety goat houses. I walked carefully in the ruts the tires made, on guard for something else to jump at me. Mr. Coleman owned a nice stretch of land, but like children of the depression he never threw anything away, ever. In previous years, he had raised rabbits and poultry as evidenced by an elaborate, but now unused and dilapidated, system of coups and cages. Now in his twilight years, he was down to three rabbits, a dozen chickens, and one Aflac duck.

I should probably pause here to say that when I initially volunteered to work for goat manure I assumed that meant shoveling from inside the four walls of Billy's barn, preferably in the shade. What I couldn't know was that sometime in the spring, before I'd met either gentleman, Billy had promised Mr. Coleman he would clean out his goat houses.

"I like to help the elderly," Billy said as he tossed the first of many shovels full of manure into the back of the truck.

Mr. Coleman is ninety-years-old. Billy is seventy-seven. I suspected before the day was done, I'd feel older than both of them combined.

It's amazing how hot you get while lifting a manure laden shovel. Despite a gentle breeze, sweat trickled down the small of my back. My chest hurt. I gasped for breath. I was out of shape. The tiny pebble-like goat droppings had seasoned to a powdery consistency that rendered the pitchfork I'd brought useless. Billy placed a shovel in my hand. The wind seemed to blow each time I heaved a shovelful into the back of the truck. Soon manure flecks dotted my face. Beads of sweat gathered at my temple, mingled with the manure and trickled down my face leaving a dirty trail that curved around my jaw and dripped off the tip of my chin. Just when I thought I was going to have a heart attack, Billy called break time. I leaned against my shovel and sucked the water bottle until the insides touched.

"Why does Mr. Coleman have so many gates?" I asked.

Billy wiped his brow with the back of his hand and responded, "When you got goats, you gotta rotate their pasture." He gestured to the lot behind us. "See how they've stripped everything down to the ground. It's almost time to turn them loose on another patch of land. After a while, they'll have this eat up. The gate we passed at the entrance surrounds his vegetable garden."

"You mean he still works a garden?" I asked.

Billy nodded and said, "Several folks come help him grow a garden. Couple people used to keep their horses in here too."

I looked around at the weeds that were higher than my head. Either goat manure made everything grow speedy quick, or the workers had quit in the middle of the summer.

With much effort, a large pile of the black gold pellets accumulated in the back of the truck. There was enough to fertilize all my plants. I threw the shovel on top of the manure and headed toward the passenger side of the truck.

Billy laughed. "We're not done," he said. "I've got to clean out *all* the goat houses today."

My first thought was, "If I lift this shovel one more time, I'm going to die." Instead I said, "Okey dokey."

This was one of those times I wished I had my camera. Somehow Billy bent at the waist and entered a house built for a small goat. Picture a six-foot tall man entering a medium-sized dog house. Since I was the smaller of the two, it only made sense I go inside with the shovel, but he'd have none of it. I soon learned why. The manure was packed hard. Billy hacked at it with the mattock while I rested against the truck and regained my breath. All too soon he tossed out large chunks of manure that I heaved into the truck.

An hour later, we stopped.

"Looks like we're done," he announced.

I wanted to say "God yeah," but was too tired to speak.

I piled into the truck trying not to inhale the scent of myself as Billy drove the burdened truck home down the pig trail. I unlocked the gate and said goodbye to a different time. I couldn't help but chuckle as we traveled through the affluent residential district past homes with million-dollar price tags leaving clods of goat manure scattered along the way.

Chapter Eight

The "Honer" System

"I like to trust people, and I believe people like to be trusted."
—Billy Albertson

At a time when those we've entrusted with our money have betrayed our confidence, stolen our retirement funds, and left us feeling angry and bitter, Billy provides a Christian example of honesty and integrity. He believes in order to gain a person's trust one must first trust them. This simple concept leaves me wondering, can people really be trusted, or are people in general looking for the first opportunity to take something from me?

A white trashcan liner stretched across a piece of wood with the word "Tomatoes" written in black sharpie serves as a sign. This hand-made beacon entices more people than any flashing neon billboard ever could. It's hard to imagine that someone could make a living farming in an area within walking distance of million-dollar homes and a high school foot-ball field equipped with a Jumbo-tron.

The table inside his carport is heavy with vegetables: tomatoes, beans, cucumbers, squash, and if the good Lord's willing, okra and corn. The words "Honer System please serve yourself. Thanks, Billy . . . PS closed on Sunday," are written across a piece of paper. Another sign marked, "Money Barrell" is taped to a faded Charles Potato Chip bucket. Certified scales hang from the carport ceiling. Recycled grocery bags are crammed inside a cardboard box. Their tiny plastic handles waving in the warm summer breeze.

Billy isn't embarrassed about the misspelled words and mismatched signs. He'll be the first to say he only has a seventh grade education, saying, "I got my education out behind the barn."

Meaning, he received his fair share of spankings. He feels no shame that he didn't graduate high school. I imagine the bigger shame would be if he grumbled and expected a handout because he lacks schoolin'. Billy has always earned a living by the sweat of his brow. Some may laugh and call him backward and uneducated, but a man who works hard and has the calluses to prove it, has my admiration and respect.

Those who gauge intelligence based on college degrees and income earning potential would be surprised to discover how well Billy manages his farm. Over the years, he's enticed many customers with a variety of signs. One day he noticed me eyeballing a red tomato-shaped sign constructed from piece of plywood, "My grandson Matthew made that."

I imagine that sign is too precious for use. Besides, he believes simple is best. So for now, he uses trashcan liners and plates with scratched out letters.

Here's how the "Honer System" works. If Billy isn't in the carport when customers arrive he's working in the garden or tending the critters. The customers select the vegetables they wish to purchase from the table. Tomatoes are pre-bagged and weighed. Beans and peas are sold by the pound. Squash and cucumbers are sold loose, usually three or five for a dollar depending on their size. Calculate the amount owed using the price list taped to the table. Place the money in the potato chip bucket marked "Money Barrell." If customers don't have the exact amount, they can make change from the loose dollars and coins inside the "Money Barrell." It really is that simple.

As I surveyed the vegetable stand, Billy read the look on my face.

"What prevents someone from coming in and stealing vegetables and all the money?" I asked.

Billy leaned in close, his voice low and said, "I believe people need to be trusted. I like to be trusted." He paused, then inched closer, "don't you like to be trusted?"

I nodded. He's right. The ultimate insult is to imply that I lack honesty or integrity.

"So, if you treat people like you can trust them, guess what, you can" he said.

When I grow up, I want to be just like Billy. Sometimes his wisdom leaves me shaking my head. I wonder, when did the invisible shift in integrity happen? When did people start caring more about themselves, filling their lives with expensive things, unable to see the suffering of others? And more important, will they continue to serve themselves and ignore the needy?

According to the most recent United States census, one in four households consists of one person. Coupled with emailing, instant messaging, and texting instead of face-to-face conversations, the United States is becoming a nation of lonely people. I'm not saying that all people who live alone are lonely, but there is a shifting from a community that looks after each other, to individuals opting to fulfill personal needs instead of reaching out to someone who may be hurting.

Not too long ago, people visited their neighbors every week. The Sunday drive (after church of course), was a time to catch up with family and friends. Front porches were filled with people gossiping and discussing politics. Children scampered in the yard, caught grasshoppers and picked dandelions. They built forts and played games that encouraged individual imagination and an adventuresome spirit.

A drive through any subdivision today reveals multiple rows of beautiful homes; three story affairs with short cropped grass and lush landscapes. The occupants of the home return each afternoon, press the garage door opener and aren't seen again until the following morning. The curtains are pulled back just enough to offer a glimpse inside. The front porch gleams, shiny from lack of use. Outside, there are no children playing, no joyful laughter, no scuff marks on the steps, or rocking chair groves worn deep into the front porch. I imagine the residents living inside haven't spoken to their next-door neighbors more than twice all year.

I want to trust people and see the good in everyone like Billy does. But in the tap root of my being there's an alarm system warning me to be cautious. I'm afraid of giving my time, money, and resources to someone who is hurting. What if they steal, or try to physically hurt me? It is those fears that prevent me from being the person my heart commands. Billy gives instinctively without a second thought. When he sees a need he meets it and then goes on about his business waving off any attempt at thanks.

Maybe it's my cynical nature, but I can't help but wonder how many people take vegetables without paying. It troubles me that someone would steal from a man so generous. Trust me. It does happen. How could it not? He won't discuss it when I pry.

"What a body does is between him and God," Billy responds when I try to talk about my concerns. "Everyone's got to give an account of what they've done on this here earth."

I try to understand this live-and-let-live, leave-it-up-to-God way of thinking, but inside I want justice. I sometimes wonder if Billy's for real. Surely he can't be loving and giving *all* the time. But as I watch him extend a hand and introduce himself to complete strangers day after day, I realize that his heart is pure. He opens his home to all. He shares his animals with young and old. He has a smile and a kind word for everyone he meets. So for someone to steal from him triggers my need for justice.

"When I leave this world," Billy says with a wink, "I've got to be able to say I treated folk how I wanted to be treated. God commands me to love my neighbor. You can't hide from God. If someone wants to take a few tow-maters they've got to answer to Him. The Bible says that God knows the number of hairs on your head. He also knows your heart."

Who can argue with that? I reckon if God knows the number of hairs on my head, he knows who steals from Billy. Besides, the Bible *does* say that vengeance is the Lord's.

The "Honer System" is a mindset with roots deeper than trusting people. Billy's system means that with each bag of produce one buys, he'll get more than he pays for. When customers purchase a pound of tomatoes, they receive a "heavy pound." Meaning, the total weight is more than one pound, as opposed to an exact pound, or scant pound where the bag weighs slightly less than what's marked on the package. Today's supermarkets have perfected the weighing process to the ounce. If customers purchase three pounds of produce at Billy's odds are they'll come home with three and a quarter.

I worry about Billy, and I'm not the only one. His good friend Kay Hambright stopped by one afternoon to deliver a meal. People are always doing that, delivering meals, inviting him to dinner, trying to follow his example. On this particular afternoon Mrs. Hambright arrived bearing dinner. The house was unlocked. Billy's car was in the driveway. She opened the door and called. No answer. She stepped into the shed, and then the barn. No Billy. She waited for a moment her concern building with each tick of the clock. She placed the food inside and made the call. She left a note which read: "Billy, I brought you dinner but you weren't home. I waited but you never showed up. I was worried and called the police. Kay Hambright."

By chance, I was passing by and noticed the unmistakable piercing flash of blue lights. Two patrol cars were parked askew in Billy's driveway.

"Momma," Jamie said, "something's happened."

My heart sank. I immediately thought the worst. I imagined his body mangled and bloody lying on the kitchen floor. Someone had broken in, I reasoned and stolen . . . what? Plastic containers and chickens? Billy doesn't own material things. His clothes are patched. His boots are duct taped together. Even his tools are rusty and worn. I didn't want to alarm my daughter, but I needed to know what was going on. I parked the car and was approached by a police officer.

"Ma'am, Do you know the man who lives here?" He asked. His tone was dull. His words were short and to the point.

I swallowed hard and nodded.

"Mrs. Hambright has reported him missing. Are you his daughter?"

I shook my head and said, "No sir, I am not. I drop by several times a week to help out." I turned to find Doyle, Billy's next door neighbor, speaking to another officer. I nodded a greeting but he didn't acknowledge it. His face was masked with worry. I placed a hand on my stomach, hoping to steady the churning acid.

Officer Nolan opened a small notepad exactly like you see in the movies. "Ma'am can you tell me the last time you saw Mr. Albertson?" he asked.

I answered his questions while we walked the property. "Did you check the barn?" I asked.

He nodded and said, "I didn't go inside." I pointed to Jamie who took off in a run.

"Be sure you look around good, in case he fell and can't call out for help," I called as she entered the goat pasture.

Officer Nolan and I searched the remaining outbuildings. No Billy.

"Have you checked the corn field?" I asked.

"Yes Ma'am, we walked all the rows," he responded.

"No, sir, I mean the field across from the church. He also has corn planted there. Maybe he's there." I said hopefully.

Officer Nolan spoke into the radio on his shoulder, dispatching another officer to the field. I tried not to panic.

"Have you been inside the house?" I paused for a moment uncertain whether to continue. "I don't know how to ask, but were their any signs of a struggle?" I continued.

"We have searched the residence," he replied without answering my question.

At that moment, Billy's younger daughter Denise arrived. Her face wet with tears. Her words were filled with panic as she explained that her dad had gone with someone to a lodge meeting, but both should have been back by now. She called the lodge and was told that Billy had left a few hours ago.

It appeared that he had vanished.

"Has your Dad ever wandered off?" Officer Nolan asked Denise.

She shook her head no, and wiped her eyes. We all felt helpless. Where could he be?

By now cars were slowing down along the busy road. One turned in and Billy stepped out. In typical Billy Albertson style he approached, extended his hand and asked, "Officer, what's a going on here?"

"Sir, we're looking for the man who lives here. Do you know anything about him?" the officer asked.

That loveable spirit dwelling inside Billy revealed a broad smile. He extended his hand toward the officer and said, "Why I shore do. You're a looking at him."

Billy's daughters were angry after he'd given everyone such a scare. He laughed it off saying, "I knowed where I was all along."

The police have added Billy's house to their list of weekly stops. Even officers patrolling a major metropolis crave the magical experience Billy provides. They stop in "just to check on things," chat for a moment and leave with a smile.

It's hard knowing what's best. I too was concerned, and thought the worst. Since Billy doesn't own a cell phone, I don't think he could have done anything to prevent Mrs. Hambright's panic. Billy had returned from the lodge as he said he would; however, moments later someone invited Billy to go for a road trip. Billy "keeps the roads hot" visiting folk. He travels much more than I do, checking in on folk in the nursing homes and hospitals.

When the visitin' bug hits one must get in the car. Even at seventy-seven years old, I don't think Billy's social calendar should be controlled by anyone. He's got a long way to go before he's as absentminded as, oh . . . let's just say me for example.

Today, there's a note on the door which reads, "Check the Barn." It also has my cell phone number, and both daughters' numbers listed. If neighbors stop by with a home-cooked meal and find the house empty, please call one of us instead of bothering the police. He may be off visitin'.

Chapter Nine

Here We Go 'Round
The Money Tree

"Reckon if a body had a field of these trees planted,
he'd never have to work again."
—Billy Albertson

We were returning to the garden after eating a bite of lunch when I saw movement in the garden to my right. Billy had planted field corn near the goat pasture in an area surrounded by wire fencing. Later he'd planted cucumbers between the corn. Their sturdy stalks provided support as bright green tendrils corkscrewed up the plant, inching toward the sun releasing leaves that effectively enclosed the property in a massive wall of green. I stood for a moment, half expecting to discover a hawk plucking feathers from a chicken, or a crow eating corn. I watched in amazement as a goat squeezed through the fence gate, followed by another, and another. Like locusts they attacked the garden, consuming everything in their path.

"Billy," I yelled while running toward the corn. "The goats are in the garden!"

I pushed my weight into the first goat. I pressed hard, using every ounce of strength to move the small animal. The stubborn-willed creature turned to look at me, a stalk still in its mouth, but refused to budge.

I think it smiled.

Billy, who'd witnessed everything from the kitchen window, dashed barefoot across the field and grabbed the first goat he met by the horns. "Get on outta here," he said while giving the animal a quick tug. "That Daisy's the ringleader. She leads these other goats into trouble every time."

He reached for another goat and yelled, "Zippy, guard the gate to make sure nobody gets back in."

I tried, oh how I tried to make sure the goats stayed in the pasture where they belonged, but somehow a renegade made a run for the money tree. If I've learned anything about goats, it's that there's always a non-conformist in the herd.

I was unfamiliar with *Ficus Carica*, commonly known in Georgia as the fig tree. Growing up in the western North Carolina mountains, I naively assumed figs were native to tropical climates or perhaps Florida.

I graciously declined the fig when he'd first presented me with the miniature pear-shaped fruit.

"I don't think I like them," I said like a child whose just been offered spinach. Truth be told, the closest I'd come to tasting a fresh fig was opening a new box of Fig Newtons.

"Aw come on," he said while breaking the fruit in half and pushing it under my nose. "They're good for you."

I examined it. The pale yellow-green skin protected pink flesh which contained about a million seeds. I took a tiny bite as he watched, silently wondering how in the world I would spit the seeds out and not hurt his feelings. Instead, I was surprised. Remarkably, the fruit was delicious, seeds and all.

"Here, have another. You look like you need all the energy you can get," Billy said.

During the small window of harvest, Billy paid me in figs. Soon even my finicky daughter was eating them. I even began slipping them into my husband's fruit smoothie in place of sweetener.

With prices topping $6.00 a pound in the grocery store, the fruit from this glorious deciduous tree is prized. Billy's tree produces two crops. If the weather cooperates and there are no spring cold snaps, the tree yields a bountiful crop which Billy's clientele' quickly devours. In fact folk begin asking for figs in June and continue their search long after the tree is bare.

"The fig tree!" I yelled.

I abandoned the gate and dashed toward the tree, hoping it wouldn't be stripped bare before I got there.

Figs are delicate and highly fragile. While some crops need rain to mature, this fruit will sour and rot if rainfall is abundant. Unlike Georgia's peach crop, immature figs will not ripen off the tree. They are only picked when ripe and should be enjoyed immediately. Because the flesh is delicate and bruises easy, they can't be harvested and allowed to sit in the summer heat waiting for a customer who may or may not come along. For those reasons, customers who arrive at Billy's are sent directly to the source. Figs are the only pick-your-own crop on his farm. However, this applies to humans only, not goats.

While Billy shepherded the goats out of the corn and into their rightful place, I gave chase to the renegade. I bent at the knee and extended my arms. Like a Peacock, I made myself as large as possible. Then I advanced. The goat lowered her head, flashed two life-taking horns, and called my bluff.

After the first round the score read:

Goat: One

Zippy: Zero

I grabbed a rake and tried again. This time she ran around the tree and resumed plucking the fruit. I considered my options.

"Here, let me give you a hand," Billy said from behind me. "You go around that side; I'll come around the left."

He grabbed the renegade by the horns and gave a tug. She tugged back, but he was persistent. Her back hooves dug furrows in the dirt as he closed the gate with a clang.

A thick three-ring notebook, its pages curled toward the sun, rested at the corner of the table. He grabbed the portable phone and carefully dialed the first number listed. "Let's see if I can get some customers in here."

"You want some figs?" He asked the moment someone answered on the other end. He didn't introduce himself. I suspect there's only one person who'd be calling to ask this question. "The figs are ready now. I'm going to call a few other folk."

That's his way of saying if you don't come now they'll be gone. And customers do come, quickly. They pick by the handfuls, bringing baskets, and using shirttails, chatting excitedly about the harvest and their plans for the fruit.

The money tree requires little maintenance. It doesn't need watering except in times of severe drought. A miniscule amount of fertilizer is required. Too many nutrients in the soil and the tree explodes with growth, but yields smaller fruit. It's a lazy man's crop requiring only patience and full sun. Unlike most fruit trees a harvest can be enjoyed soon after planting, which makes it the perfect tree for my parents who don't have a lot of time to tend fruit crops.

"You think you could root me a money tree?" I asked.

Billy removed his pocketknife. "Only one way to find out," he answered.

He made a tiny cut in a low hanging limb. I took the shovel and disturbed a small area of dirt beneath the tree. He placed the limb in the dirt while I covered it with soil. He held the limb in place with a brick. With any luck, I'll transplant a little bit of Billy's garden into theirs. They'll be thrilled.

Chapter Ten

Waste Not Want Not

"If I can't take care of what I got, then why do I need something new?"
—**Billy Albertson**

Billy Albertson grew up in a large family during a time when people made do with what they had. He describes the family dynamics this way, "the family had seven boys and each of those boys had four sisters."

Maybe it was growing up as a child of the depression that created a frugal lifestyle, or having a large family where everything was shared that encouraged Billy to appreciate what he has. Billy often tells me, "We didn't have nothing growing up."

I beg to differ.

They didn't have video games, cell phones, or even television. He wore hand me down clothes layered with patches instead of designer name brands. His feet were clad with mended socks and crammed inside his brother's resoled boots. He listened to music . . . live. He began each day milking the cow, then went to school. Afterward, he did chores until sunset. He never uttered the words, "I'm bored." Back then, neighbors knew each other. Billy was respectful and honored his parents by never talking back. He continues today with every person he meets. To put it another way, even though he grew up without material things, his home was rich.

America's vast consumerism has come a long way since the time when nothing was wasted. I'm not certain when we lost our way, or more importantly, if we'll ever cast off our feeling of entitlement. Hopefully, with the green movement, combined with the far-reaching effects of economic crisis, American's are slowly changing their habits. Clothes we no longer wear, toys the children are bored with, old cell phones, all can be reused.

In Billy's day, clothes were mended until the holes were too large to hold patches. Then, instead of being thrown away, the cloth was cut into pieces and stitched together for quilts. He doesn't follow the rest of the world's disposable behavior. He rarely requires new things. For example, the tools in his shed are over forty years old. Billy's thinking, "If I can't take care of what I've got, then why do I need something new?"

Billy generates virtually no trash. Even chicken feed bags are reused until they are threadbare. I've incorporated some of his lifestyle techniques into my household. In the days before Billy I tossed kitchen scraps into the garbage disposal. Today, I'm going green (I guess) by keeping a small bucket beside my trashcan. All household scraps from banana peels, to those inedible homemade biscuits I keep making, go into the bucket. Once a week I take the scraps to his chickens who now welcome me like a family pet. Billy tells me I've spoiled them. This from the man who feeds them grass clippings; cutting the lawn for the chickens, now that's spoiling the birds.

I've changed the way I recycle plastic bags. Most grocery stores encourage shoppers to bring their own bags. I do not. I take used bags to Billy.

"Law, you've brought me some sacks. I sure do need 'em," Billy said the first time I delivered a load of bags. "You know these are as rare as hen's teeth."

I don't know about hen's teeth, but I do know plastic bags are vital to his produce stand. He keeps a large cardboard box full of recycled bags in a lawn chair at the corner of the shed. In my inexperience, I believed there were enough bags to last all summer. In reality, they were gone in a week. Not too long ago, he needed bags and I considered robbing the recycling container at Publix. Fortunately, a customer brought some "sacks" as he calls them, that she'd been saving all winter. Still, should Atlantans pass an older man driving a beat up get away truck with plastic bags flapping in the breeze, please don't call the law. We're just desperate for some sacks.

Instead of labeling Billy a pack rat, I call him the man who has it all.

"I don't throw nothin' away," he's said to me more than once.

Discontinued, hard-to-find parts, pieces and products are tucked inside his shed, "just in case someone needs it." If Billy doesn't have it, odds are, he'll know someone who does. Farmers need a miscellany of equipment, tools, buckets, and fertilizers to break ground and plant crops. Those who also raise livestock need odd items we discard every day like: egg cartons, grocery bags, plastic and glass containers and table scraps. Billy's ability to use what most throw away is remarkable, which is why I bring him odd shaped pieces of lumber, empty buckets and fresh baked chocolate chip cookies . . . even Billy has vices.

Going green is not a new concept for Billy. He's been that way most of his life. He appreciates the generosity of others. Someone else's trash truly is his treasure. As a result, he accepts everything I accumulate. I've carried all sorts of things to his house. I've even raked leaves and pulled scrub pine saplings from my yard to feed his goats. And regardless of what I bring, he never treats my things like trash. To him, each item is welcomed and used.

Long before electricity and indoor plumbing, women set aside one day each week for "washing."

"Mother would use three kettles," Billy explained. "She'd build the fire real hot under the biggest pot she had. She'd put some lye soap and bluing in the water, then she'd boil the clothes."

A puzzled look crossed my face. "What's bluing?" I asked.

"Bluing is an additive she put in the water to purify the clothes," Billy answered.

"Wait a minute. Didn't all the clothes turn blue?" I asked.

With a long suffering amount of patience, he explained. "Bluing turned the water a dark blue color. Instead of being a fabric dye like you'd see today, it made your white clothes the whitest white you've ever seen."

Since I wear the dingiest clothes imaginable, this bluing additive intrigued me. The more I bleach my whites, the dingier they become. "Where can you get it?" I asked.

"Law, I don't know, prolley don't make it no more," he said.

I was disappointed that he didn't have a jar of the bluing laying around in the shed.

He continued: "The clothes would boil, and Mother would soak them and let them purify for a while. Then she moved them to another pot and let them rinse. She had an assembly line going. After all the clothes were wrung out and hung on the line she'd let the fire die down in the first kettle. Then my brothers would get in and wash."

I held up my hand to stop him. "Hold up. Are you telling me ya'll bathed in the blue water?" I asked.

His head tilted toward the sky. Deep dimples appeared in his cheeks as his heart released a laugh so contagious I had to join. "Oh yeah. Then my

61

sisters would wash. By the end of the day Mother was so tired my sisters would bathe me in that blue water," he said.

Kind of makes me understand the importance of water today. Especially when I consider that every drop used back then was carried by hand. And I complain when I have to do the laundry. Talk about spoiled.

"Each summer our well used to go dry," he said. "You know it was just a hand-dug well, so in the summer we'd bathe in the creek. I liked it better than the wash pot. Back then I despised a bath, but now, I'd rather do without money, than water."

As the son of a sharecropper, Billy also learned that water is precious. Water was the lifeblood of the growing process. Without it there were no crops, and without crops a lot of mouths would go hungry. The same holds true today, even if people won't admit it.

Billy's property is sprinkled with water barrels. He doesn't own fancy containers with pipes running from the roof. Instead, fifty-five gallon trash cans sit at the drip line on all four corners of his house, shed, and other out buildings. Anytime the garden needs a drink he dips a plastic bucket into the water. His system also attracts mosquitoes.

It pains me to watch as he dips buckets into the green water writhing with larvae then lug heavy the burdensome buckets from plant to plant for the sole purpose of watering thirsty vegetables. In my heart I want Billy to have a real rain barrel. A fancy citified system which would be enclosed to keep out dangerous blood sucking mosquitoes. I worry about him falling, or worse, stepping in an uneven spot and breaking a bone while carrying buckets of water. In my mind I have designed the perfect water reclamation system. It's a thing of beauty. Three fifty-five gallon plastic drums will sit atop a waist-high wooden platform with his antiquated wheelbarrows parked beneath. I'll install these containers and rig them with nozzles and hoses. The water would be safely enclosed in plastic, permanently solving the mosquito problem. Of course a hosepipe would snake directly into the garden. Just two things stand in my way of this vision, Billy Albertson and opportunity.

It's nigh on impossible to surprise this man, especially with anything that involves construction on his property. He leaves the house on certain days, for particular events, but rarely spends enough time away to complete a project of this magnitude. If I'm going to install a rain barrel as a covert surprise mission, I must enlist the help of his daughters or tell him my plans.

Billy does more than reclaim rainwater. He is a careful steward of every drop. Each side of the kitchen sink features a plastic container. He fills one side with soapy water, the other clear. Throughout the day he uses this water for dish and hand washing. While some may think his technique unsanitary, I disagree. Water is a precious resource that he uses wisely. When he was a child, water wasn't the only resource wisely used.

"After Mother finished the laundry," Billy said, "she'd gather the ashes and make lye soap. I don't know how she made it, but I remember helping her scoop up the ashes."

Even today the ashes from his fireplace are sprinkled on his garden. It's cheaper than buying potash.

As I watched Billy use every ounce of water with painful efficiency, I pondered my wasteful habits and was ashamed. In 2008, Georgia experienced a historic drought. The governor and local officials announced tight restrictions and people were urged to conserve. I pestered my husband until he installed a rain barrel at our home, but that wasn't enough. I could do more. Low flow toilets were the rage, but came with a hefty price tag for our older multi-bathroom home. Instead, I placed a quart jar of water inside the commode's holding tank. With each flush, the volume of water it takes to refill the tank is decreased, not significantly, but every little bit helps.

Copying Billy's kitchen technique, I've placed a plastic bowl in the sink. I capture the water I use while washing my hands. I still run the dishwasher, but instead of pre-rinsing dishes I swirl them around in the bowl before loading. I then use the dirty water (called gray water), on thirsty flowers. I don't worry about detergent in the water. I pour the gray water in a circular pattern around each plant, never on the leaves. I believe it establishes a barrier those pesky insects don't want to cross.

I never irrigate my lawn, ever. Most people don't realize the more you water plants the more they need. Many gardeners have bought into the methodology that lawns and gardens must be watered daily when that isn't the truth. The Georgia Department of Agriculture confirms that frequently watered flora produce tiny, shallow roots that are dependent on irrigation; however, plants that aren't sprinkled daily send forth massive roots deep into the ground searching for water, effectively creating a healthier lawn and garden.

Billy also applies two to three inches of mulch around his vegetables. A visit to his garden will reveal tomato plants with mounds of mulch at the base. This ensures the roots are kept cool and every drop of water is captured and sent to the plant instead of evaporating.

The shower is another area where I am conserving. Governor Perdue asked Georgians to conserve by taking shorter showers. Since women require longer showers, for all that shaving, conditioning, and grooming it takes to make us beautiful, my new routing involves me washing my hair, applying conditioner then turning the water off. I shave my legs, and then turn the shower back on for a quick rinse. I estimate I save at least a gallon of water per shower.

While I'm no Billy Albertson, if each person used resources as wisely as he does, the world might be a better place.

Chapter Eleven

Sharp Knives

"A good man always carries a pocket knife."
—Renea Winchester

While stepping between the chicken house and the entrance to the goat pasture, I noticed a large stone wheel with a metal handle. The worn tool was attached to the corner of the building. I chuckled and thought: *that thing looks like it came from the set of the Flintstones.* I looked at the tool, checked to make sure no one was watching, then dared to touch the handle and give it a turn. Probably an antiquated corn sheller, I guessed, then went on about my business. I was wrong. Billy had worked for many years as a butcher. The tool was a grinder used in knife sharpening.

Let me pause for a moment to relive a childhood memory. My father often carried a tiny rectangular whetstone in his pocket which he calls a "whit-rock." The stone is used to keep knives razor sharp. Years ago, carrying a knife didn't cause concern, but forgetting it on the dresser did. Simply put, good men carried pocket knives . . . city boys didn't. Even today, Dad is never without his pocket knife. He uses it to cut everything from sticks to those blasted plastic-wrapped, plastic-tied, tripled-taped containers that manufacturers insist on using to package everything we purchase.

Hearing about Billy's former life as a butcher was all it took for me to launch into action. I can't tell you how many times I have announced that "my knives are dull." Does anyone sharpen my knives? Alas, they remain dangerous. Dull knives, which require extra force to chop, dice and slice, are unsafe. I don't have to describe to the culinary gifted how important sharp implements are in the kitchen. The old saying is true, "A dull knife will cut you quicker than a sharp one." And now I had unlimited access to a knife sharpening expert. I was thrilled. The following day I arrived at Billy's with a cardboard box. I placed it on the table and pronounced that today was "sharpening day."

"Okay," he said in a childlike tone that made me smile.

He gathered my knives and tested the sharpness of each one with his thumb. I haven't figured out why one tests the sharpness of a knife this way. My dad does it, as did his Dad before him. A frown lined Billy's face. "Boy, you sure brought these to the right place," he said. "They're a dull mess."

He picked up my favorite knife, the one with a bent tip and asked, "What happened here?"

Incapable of telling a lie, I said, "I tried to separate frozen hamburger patties."

He chuckled. "Looks like it didn't work out for ya."

"Which is why I brought it to you," I said with a laugh. "There's more where that came from at home."

"Let me get to work then," he said with a grin.

I mistakenly thought he'd use a whit-rock like my dad. To my surprise, he gathered a variety of tools and laid them on the table. He carried the bent-blade knife to the grinding wheel and turned the crank. I reached out to turn the wheel, but he shook his head. There must be a certain method of applying pressure while turning the handle that allows only experienced sharpeners to operate this machinery. I figured if I turned the wheel while he held the blade to the stone, the process would go faster.

Billy reminds me that faster isn't always better. I'm trying to understand the concept, but keep interrupting myself. I'm always in a hurry. I thrash around from task to task, in his words, "like a chicken with its head cut off." A shocking, but accurate image, as any headless creature be it man, or chicken, has trouble knowing which direction to turn.

The rapid passing of time became apparent the moment I learned of Mother's cancer. Instead of enjoying life, I make lists of things I must accomplish. I rush through the day, mentally checking things off knowing I won't get everything done. I fall into bed exhausted and frustrated that tomorrow brings another day and another incomplete list.

The grinder made an annoying bumping sound as it contacted the chipped edges of metal. He tested the blade again, shook his head slightly, then abandoned the wheel to retrieve another tool. I followed like a hungry goat begging for an ear of corn.

66

I couldn't wait to tell Dad about this experience. I'm trying to give both parents equal telephone time. I know that my parents aren't telling me everything about Mom's health. My first clue was when she said, "You may have to spend the summer with us." Her statement did nothing to alleviate the cumbersome guilt I already lugged around. Dad overheard our conversation and pulled me aside.

"It's my job to take care of your mother," he said. His tone was firm.

But I don't want it to be. I want to make things better, for everyone. I want to be a good mother, wife, and daughter. In my heart I know I could be everything to everyone if I just lived closer. I know Dad feels helpless. One of his gifts is the ability to fix anything. By anything I mean absolutely anything that is broken or in need of repair. From heat pumps to hot water heaters, flat tires to dilapidated dishwashers, his is the gift of repair. Only this time he can't fix what's broken inside my mother. This time, he is helpless.

Instead of moving in, I visit. I make short, prodigal-daughter visits that make everyone feel better. I arrive, arms heavy with groceries and gifts. I cook, clean, and carry stories from the farm which entertains my parents. Each time I arrive Dad grabs me tight and lifts me into the air in an embrace that wordlessly reveals his fears. He hugs me as if I were two-years-old absorbing my love as I collect his concerns. His pale blue eyes say, "Thank God you're here. Please don't leave."

Billy held the wooden handle of a circular file in his left hand, and pressed the tip of it against his ribcage. His right hand pushed out and sliced the dull knife across the file with a clank. He flicked his wrist, turned the knife and pulled it toward his stomach. His pace quickened and the knife began to hiss as it approached his midsection. I watched in alarm and held my breath as Billy broke my father's number one knife sharpening rule.

Never point a knife toward your body.

Clank . . . hiss. Clank . . . hiss. Metal against metal. One hard and unmoving, the other dull, becoming sharp. The third a precious man whose friendship keeps me sane.

The blade flashed, almost smiling as a new edge formed. He laid the file on the table, held the knife in one hand and with the other touched his thumb to the blade. He nodded then placed the knife on the table, "I'll be right back," Billy said as he walked to the garage where he stores a variety of tools I'll never learn to operate.

This time, a rectangular whit-rock was in his left hand. I almost laughed. Finally, this I remembered.

"Now that tool I recognize," I said as he unzipped the pocket of his overalls and fished out a small bottle of honing oil. "Until now, I didn't know what kind of gizmos you've been using."

Billy laughed. "Sometimes if you want things done right you've got to pull out all the tools," he said.

He placed the small stone on the table and added a microscopic drop of oil. The knife made a swishing sound as he moved it back and forth, first one side, then the other. He leaned over and pressed down hard, arguing with the ornery tip, forcing the last non-conforming curled edge into submission. By now, the blade was so sharp I could see the bevel from where I stood.

He stopped, held the knife to the sky and examined it. Sunlight bounced across the steel as he studied the point. His thumb touched the blade once more. He nodded then unbuttoned his shirtsleeve and rolled two cuffs. Emotion pressed hard into the chamber of my heart as an image replayed. I cringed and pulled my shoulders toward my chest while bending my head to one side. I knew what came next. I'd seen this as a child. The testing technique bothered me then, it bothers me still. Billy straightened his arm and drew the knife across his skin creating a bare place. My eyes stung. My heart hurt. His manner was familiar, reminding me of people who are no longer in my life.

As the sun flashed across my face, for a moment my grandfather is alive. It's a Sunday afternoon, church is over. The "dinner" dishes have been cleaned and put away. I'm playing with my cousins aware of adult conversations which travel on thick puffs of exhaled cigarette smoke. It's my time to hide in the yard. Grandpa sits on the front porch in his cane-back chair telling stories, as was his way; loud half-truths filled with spontaneous, contagious laughter. From my hiding place beneath the rhododendron I hear him say, "My knife's so sharp you can shave with it."

The image of Grandpa is so clear I can almost smell the cigarettes. He rolls his pants up two cuffs revealing thin, pasty legs. He opens the knife. The clicking sound is loud, with a hint of danger. I stare, mouth open, as he scrapes the blade across his bony shin. Hairs tumble to the porch where they are picked up by the wind and disappear from sight.

I smiled at the memory, while tears pooled. The loss is still more than I can bear. The bittersweet pain serves as a reminder of the hole he left that even Billy can't fill. Everyone I know, friends, family, even the casual acquaintance, breathes life into who I am. When one of these precious creations leaves me I feel a loss most people can't understand.

I gather experiences. I capture memories of time, snapshots of moments that escape and dance across my mind without warning or explanation. Most people will admit they want to be remembered after they die. A legacy, if you will, that their life mattered to someone. We want our name mentioned years after we exhale our last breath. If I have known someone, even casually, part of them is inside of me. I will worry when they become ill. I will send cards of encouragement. I will pray. I will mourn when I read their obituary and hurt when they depart this earth. That is my gift, and my curse. I don't forget people placed in my path.

Remembrances flash in my mind. I will remember things about them at odd, unexplained times. A moment I have gathered will replay. In my mind, I will recall what they wore, how they looked, and possibly, even what was said. I do not forget people God has placed in my path, that I can promise.

My remembrances come without warning as was the case when a red-tailed hawk appeared outside my door. Leon Jones is an example of someone I lost whose face I can clearly remember. He was Chief of the Eastern Band of Cherokee Indians from 1999 to 2003. One spring afternoon we were gathered atop a majestic mountaintop in the Great Smoky Mountains National Park, encouraging donations to the Friends of the Smokies charity. We stood beside each other staring into the valley that was filled with the lush green tapestry of spring. The wind, erratic and forceful, caressed our faces as we stood together sharing no words, only the sky, the clouds, the earth.

Slowly, Chief Jones turned. His dark brown eyes looked past me, ignoring my presence. He smiled, lifted his arms and reached toward the sky. I looked beyond the end of his fingertips. A red-tailed hawk floated above us, wings stretched wide, capturing warm puffs of air. It glided without effort, without sound, turning and dipping, teasing and diving toward the man with outstretched hands.

"Ta-wo-di," he whispered, calling the creature using the words of the Cherokee.

It came to him, circled high above his head as I stood amazed. Bird and man seemed connected. The Chief's head tilted back, eyes wide as both hands reached toward the creature beckoning it to come to him. The hawk looked down at the man below whose silver hair blew in the wind. It circled him once . . . then a second time and was gone.

"Wow," I gushed. "I've never seen anything like that before."

"That's my ta-wo-di . . . my hawk," he said in a tone which left no doubt. "My grandmother conjured him to me when I was a child. She told me that I should search for my ta-wo-di everywhere I go. He watches over me, protecting me from harm."

I suspect when Chief Jones died, the hawk reached down with powerful talons and captured his precious spirit then carried it to heaven.

Today, watching Billy sharpen my knives fills me with longing for my grandpa. The emptiness I feel is unbearable. Yes, I'll remember Billy. I'll remember him when I bite into a ripe tomato. Others I'll recall when a hawk passes overhead whispering their name, or when I see naked skin appear beneath a freshly sharpened knife.

Chapter Twelve

Goats and Other Livestock

"Mercy, you've got a lotta goats."
—Renea Winchester

Soon after Billy built his house, he fenced in a pasture for the milk cow named Bossy. A true recycler, he relocated a barn from his neighbor's property across the street and reconstructed it at the corner of his property. Today, the barn still stands. He and wife Marjorie milked Bossy twice a day. In addition to drinking the milk, Marjorie churned butter and made buttermilk that the family used. Bossy was bred and each spring provided a calf. Billy's children, Denise and Janet, grew up enjoying the pleasures of having farm animals in their life.

It was the 60s. Many families had livestock. So many families did that a meat packing plant was located near Billy's house. Each fall, a cow was butchered providing beef for the Albertson family. Even though it pains our hearts today to know the fate of the calves, this is how life was in the 60s on a farm. Long before visionaries viewed his property as "prime real estate" suited for multi-use development, folk living outside of Atlanta used the land as God intended. They raised cotton, a small patch of sorghum cane, and a variety of animals. Many bartered for dry goods, especially when money was scarce.

"When I was growing up, Momma never let us eat eggs," Billy once told me. "The eggs were carried to town and sold to city folk. Since we did most of our trading by barter, Momma's egg money was the only spending money we had."

Billy's farming ways hold the attention of many. In 1987, Joe Earle, staff writer for the *Atlanta Journal Constitution* featured Billy in an article titled "Roswell's Urban Farmers Keep The Old Ways Despite Shrunken Pastures."

By then Maybelle had replaced Bossy as the family cow. Twenty years later, the milk cows are gone, but the farm and simple lifestyle remains.

In 2001, change came to the pasture. With the cattle gone, hedge brushes, briars, and thorny brambles were growing in the pasture faster than Billy could "knock 'em back." Because goats eat everything down to the bare earth, they were the logical solution. Billy contacted fellow farmer Oscar Goldman and the two men struck a deal. Billy took the white truck to Coleman road and returned with two pregnant nanny goats and one Billy goat. Billy's granddaughter Kristen named the female goats Princess and Nanny. The male goat she called Little Bill, after her Paw Paw.

Today, Harry, Oreo, Cookie, Daisy, and a variety of others comprise a fluctuating herd. The goats keep their master busy and teach visitors about the old ways. Twenty years after Mr. Earle's article, people are still intrigued with this tiny farm just off a busy road.

"This little strip of land has served me well," Billy said. "Even though my working days are over, I suspect I could survive on this here spot for quite sometime." Billy slips on a well-worn coat and places a cap on his hat that reminds me of Snoopy as he fights the Red Baron. "Someone's always passing through here. I like visitors."

He fills a bucket with stale bread, courtesy of a food bank. When bread reaches the expiration date it isn't discarded. Instead, this noble charity allows him to gather the stale loaves which he feeds to his goats.

"You know, I'm the luckiest man in Fulton County," he says while his steel knife slices through hard crusts with ease. "This here bread really helps me out." He cuts exotic, seed-encrusted loaves into bite-sized pieces then tosses them into a plastic bucket which he feeds to the livestock. I watch him work while the goats bleat a hungry cry.

I'm sure most people have never considered what grocery stores do with cabbage and lettuce leaves, grapes and other fruit that is past its prime. It goes into the landfill where it rots and is wasted. Billy remembers a time not too long ago when farmers helped grocery stores by taking unsold, unused food no longer fit for human consumption. Farmers fed their livestock produce we humans couldn't eat. Those days are gone. We probably have the lawyers to thank for the change in policy. Today, grocery stores won't even donate a wilted lettuce leaf for a pet rabbit.

Fortunately, many independently owned stores with deli markets choose to donate surplus bread to food banks. The greater blessing is when the charity shares the expired bread with Billy. Landfill space is saved, and animals are fed when everyone reaches out to help one another. Bread isn't the only donation he gets. A country store that receives hay by tractor trailer also extends a helping hand. Anyone who has handled hay knows that bales come unraveled. Each week Billy tosses a rake and well-used broom into the truck then travels to the store and rakes the trailer clean. The work is hard and sweaty, but his animals remain well-fed thanks to the generosity of others.

Mention goat farming and most people say, "Goats stink." Goats *are* aromatic animals, especially after a rain. Billy's goats refuse the possibility of a bath, bolting for the barn the moment the first drop falls.

"Goats pee on their beards," my mother said after I told her about Billy's animals.

While I calculated the physical difficulty of peeing on one's beard (forgive me, but I'd like to see exactly how a goat could propel a stream of urine forward without standing on his head), she elaborated that males mark their territory and themselves to entice the female sex. I will admit, during spring rains the farm does smell a bit funky; but until I see Harry-the-goat pee on his own beard I remain skeptical.

One morning I found Billy in the garage slicing breakfast for the livestock. I noticed two small goats sitting in the window frame of the building.

"That white one's momma won't let him nurse," he said before I could ask the obvious question, "why do you have baby goats in the garage?" "Someone brought him to me last night. I turned the other one in here so he wouldn't get lonely. I'm hoping to survive him."

People are always giving Billy animals they no longer want or can no longer care for. It's common for people to bring bunnies and baby goats. Unfortunately, most folk wait until the animal is in severe distress before seeking Billy's help. I looked at the tiny animal, whose gaunt body was resting against the window frame for support and asked, "Can you get one of the nannies to adopt him? Maybe Chocolate," I offered, "she's one of your better nannies."

I didn't suggest Daisy. She thinks she's people, not a nursemaid.

He shook his head and adjusted the strap of his overalls that had slipped off his shoulder. "Naw, they won't adopt another nanny's baby. But I robbed them of some milk and fed him with a dropper. I just hope he's not too far gone."

The visual of Billy corralling a nanny and milking her made me chuckle. But the situation was serious. Baby goats nurse several times an hour. We had no idea how long it had been since the little one had nursed. I could have no part of a baby goat dying. I left for the health food store where I purchased canned goat's milk.

"I don't know if this will work," I said while shaking the can. "Maybe if we dilute it a bit with water it won't hurt his tummy."

I held the tiny kid to my chest. He was lethargic. Laying his head against me as if saying, "I'm hungry and I don't have the strength to eat." Most baby goats cry out and try to escape when held, not this one. There's something about holding a baby whether human or animal, that brings out the motherly instinct in me. His legs dangled while my hips swayed as if rocking my own baby asleep. I wrapped him in my shirt and pulled him close. We managed to get some milk into him while covering ourselves in the process. I was falling in love with him.

Billy recognized my lovestruck look. "Now don't go getting attached," he warned. "We might not survive him."

The next day I arrived with a pet carrier. I had decided during the night the little kid was coming home with me. Billy shook his head and said, "I buried him this morning."

This is probably why I could never have a "real farm." I don't do death well. While I had remained naively optimistic the kid would survive, Billy knew odds weren't favorable.

My grandma often says that, "Death is a part of life." I realize this is true on every farm, but that doesn't mean I like it. Death stings the heart and hurts my soul. While Billy takes excellent care of his animals, providing the nanny's extra sweet feed during their pregnancy and postpartum period, on occasion tragedy strikes.

One might think Billy's obligations keep him home. Nothing could be further from the truth. Between the Masons, church, and community functions, he is one busy man. Such was the case the weekend he left Denise and I in charge of the farm.

It was a weekend like any other. The field was ripe for harvest. Every nanny on the farm was pregnant (I have since learned that female goats seem perpetually pregnant), the "expecting mothers" rested comfortably chewing their cud waiting for the right moment to birth their kids. Billy had cut the bread and labeled the feed buckets then reminded us to make certain everyone had plenty of water.

Once impregnated a goat gestates for five months, give or take a week. Most nannys deliver two kids weighing between four to six pounds each. Occasionally, triplets are born. Billy doesn't have time to keep a record when the kids are due, a tidbit of information that made us midwives nervous. We assured him to worry not, we could handle whatever happened and waived him away with a smile. What were the odds that any babies would be born in his absence?

It's an old wives tale that babies are born under a full moon. There was nothing special under the heavens when the kids started coming. Instead, I believe Chocolate, Blackie, Strawberry, Oreo, Silver, and Nanny, were in a race to see who could deliver first.

I had agreed to take the morning shift, and Denise would take the evening. Billy had latched the expecting mothers in the barn to keep them protected from the weather and any varmints that might want to injure a newborn. My first watch passed without any babies. Denise was the lucky one. Nanny welcomed her with a set of twins. Denise placed them in a stall and came back before dark to check on her only to find Oreo smiling with her own set of twins.

The next day was when it began to get complicated. Chocolate, Strawberry and Silver all delivered mid-day. Denise called Mark, a close friend and neighbor, who helped her move the brood safely into the nursery section of the barn. That night Blackie had triplets. All total 13 new goats were waiting for Billy when he returned. I don't think Denise or I will volunteer for nursery duty again.

Billy and Brennan planting peppers
Photo: kellemacphotography.com

Renea and Billy, Building Fences
Photo: Author

Manure: best fertilizer
in town
Photo: thecameraseye.com

Billy sharing wisdom from the
Farmer's Almanac with Brennan
Photo: kellemacphotography.com

Jamie and Madison weighing vegetables
Photo: thecameraseye.com

Billy and friends gathered
'round his truck
Photo: thecameraseye.com

Billy, Jamie and Emilie
watering tomatoes
Photo: Author

Renea and Billy
Photo: Author

King of the bucket
Photo: Author

"Money Barrell"
Photo: Author

Billy's boots
Photo: Author

Goat enjoying the sun
Photo: Author

Billy working the soil
Photo: Author

Mom, can I have a goat?
Photo: Author

Billy's Farmall cub
Photo: Author

Billy, Tristan, Kiernan and Brennan gathering hay
Photo: kellemacphotography.com

Mom, can I have a bunny?
Photo: Author

Our Angel
Photo: Author

Jamie, Future Farmer
Photo: Author

Billy covering seeds
Photo: Author

Billy, Emilie, Jamie, Matthew and Daisy
Photo: Author

Billy, Emilie, Jamie
Photo: Author

Billy checking for squash
Photo: thecameraseye.com

Chapter Thirteen

All-Timers

"You know, I can't think of nothing worse than All-Timers."
—Billy Albertson

I learned a few things about Billy while pulling weeds and plucking vegetables. He wore a wedding band, but I had never met his wife. I soon learned through eavesdropping that his wife, Marjorie, had passed away six short months before I met him. One of his daughter's had mentioned Alzheimer's and even though it was none of my business there were certain details I wanted to know about Billy's life. I wanted to ask questions, sit at his knee and listen as life experiences poured from his lips. Unfortunately, some questions are too hard to ask-or answer.

In the grayness of winter, I found him standing at the corner of the goat pasture. We chatted for a moment and he told me something he had said many times before, "These critters keep me busy." Only this time he added, "They keep my mind off my sorrow. Today I woke up bluer than the sky." Tears were forming in his eyes.

I know I'm always crying about something at Billy's, but seeing him struggle to maintain composure pained my heart. I looked at one of the baby goats and searched for the right words. But there are no words. What comfort are words when they are spoken to a man whose wife of fifty years is gone? What comfort do mere words offer to a man whose only companions now are a flock of chickens and a herd of goats? What can I offer except myself? I muddled through the moment while we watched the kids take a sip of milk from their mother.

I thought of my dad and what he'd do if, God forbid, Mother didn't defeat cancer. He's fought the battle by her side. He's driven her to the doctor, paced the hospital floors and brushed back tears he thought I didn't see.

I imagine it was divine intervention when a new neighbor moved into the brick house across from Billy back in the 80s. As the Bible commands, he extended a neighborly hand shortly after Dr. Brown unpacked. Theirs was a friendship based on respect and compassion. Dr. Brown insisted Billy call him Nelson, and Billy insisted Nelson call him friend.

In the fall of 1997, Dr. Brown made his annual house-call to the Albertson's. He'd been their unofficial doctor for years, performing physicals and administering yearly flu shots to Billy who was, "Just too busy to be bothered with doctors." On that day Billy closed the door behind them and asked Nelson if he knew anyone who could help him with Marjorie.

"Even then I knew something wasn't right," Billy said.

Billy had never uttered the word Alzheimer's in my presence. I wanted to listen without interrupting. I felt this intimate moment was fleeting and would never return. I wanted to ask about Marjorie's symptoms and how he had managed to work and care for her, the garden, and the animals. I wanted to pull information from his mouth. While my mind thought of questions to ask, common sense stepped in and whispered, "Let him talk. You won't learn anything if you don't listen."

So I listened, and my heart hurt, while he shared.

Billy told me, "Nelson could see something wasn't right with Marge. I thought she might have that sickness, but I didn't know what to do. So I asked Nelson if there was some doctor I could carry her to that could figure out what was wrong with her. He gave me the name of a doctor in downtown Atlanta. So I carried Marge to that doctor. We got there and the doctor examined her and did some blood work. He told me to take her off all medicine for two weeks then come back. They did all sorts of scans and couldn't find nothing physically wrong with her."

I nodded, imagining his anguish as he struggled to find a cure for his ailing wife.

"They prescribed Aricept. You know, that's the same medicine President Reagan took," he said.

I nodded and tried to keep my mouth shut as he shared.

Billy continued, "Back then that was just about the only medicine they had for All-Timers. I was working at the A&P and took her prescription to the pharmacist. He took one look at the paper and asked if Marge had All-Timers. I told him, 'yes.' And he said, 'Billy, you're in for a long road.'"

That was in 1997. Marge died January, 2008.

"Marge took the medicine, but it made her so sick. She'd throw up right after she took it. She stopped taking the medicine. I carried her back to the doctor and they examined her again. The doctor said he couldn't help. He told me what she needed was to see a psychiatrist. They made an appointment."

I kept quiet. This was the longest Billy had ever spoken about himself. It was difficult not to interrupt with hugs and expressions of sympathy.

He continued, "So I carried her to the psychiatrist. Now she wasn't happy, not one bit about going to the psychiatrist, but we went. The doctor examined her and gave her an antidepressant. She started taking it, but we didn't see no results. I carried her back to him a couple of times while he worked on the dose and tinkered with the medicine. Those trips got expensive, because insurance doesn't cover psychiatrist visits."

I could only imagine how expensive the treatment had been.

"Marge told me that she didn't feel no different, with or without the medicine. So she took herself off it," Billy said.

I couldn't help myself, I had to ask just one question before I exploded. "Was Marge prone to wander like other Alzheimer's patients?" I asked.

He answered, "Naw. She was always a homebody. She used to walk to the school and back, but after she got the All-Timers it was like she knew she'd forget where she lived. Instead, she wore a path around the house. She got out several times a day and walked."

Billy continued, "Eventually, Marge stopped eating. She got so skinny. For a time she weighed seventy-nine pounds. I could not get food into her. One day I was visiting my brother Bobby in the hospital. I was there to relieve my nephew for a few hours while he went to pick up his diabetic prescription. I told the nurse why I was there and she said, 'I've got something that'll cure his diabetes.' She reached in her pocket and pulled out a handful of vitamins to give to my nephew. I told her my wife has All-Timers and asked if she knew of anything that would help. 'I've got something for that too,' she said. I wrote the herbs she suggested on a piece of paper. I got Marge some Vitamin E and Ginko, and she started taking the herbs."

I pictured Billy, desperate for something that would help, willing to try anything that might restore health to his loved one.

"Did it work?" I asked.

Billy nodded and answered. "You know it did. It really helped. Marge started eating again and her weight picked back up. Since she wasn't taking any other medicine, I believe the herbs helped her a sight, until . . . "

His shoulders slumped, "Until she fell and broke her hip. She broke it good. The entire joint was broken."

I felt like I had been punched in the stomach. I wanted to scream "No!" and run from the room with my hands over my ears. I wanted to ask God why do good people like Marge, Billy, and my parents suffer?

Billy's mind was replaying her fall as if it had just happened. "The doctor showed me the x-ray. It was a complete break. He took her into surgery and repaired the hip. The doctor explained everything to me real good. He said the nurses would have her sitting up the day of the surgery. She'd be standing and taking a couple steps by the third day. So I waited and no one came to get her up. I figured the nurses knew best. It was three days before they got her up. By the time they did, she had a bedsore," he said.

I wanted to say "damn" out loud, but Billy would have scolded me, but still, "damn!"

Billy's tone had changed. He didn't have to tell me he thought Marge's bedsore was his fault. I read it in his eyes, the way he turned away from me slightly and looked beyond the goats scampering in the field. His jaw was clenched slightly, chin dropped in shame as if he had failed to properly care for her.

I said nothing. What was there to say?

"You know, I can't think of nothing worse than All-Timers," Billy said.

I had noticed little things while preparing our sandwiches in his kitchen. The plates and cups were plastic. All knives were stored far away from reach. Pots and pans were hidden inside the stove. Medication was stored on top of the refrigerator. The house was childproof and his wife was the child.

I asked, "So Billy, when Marge lost so much weight was it due to the medication, or do you think she forgot how to eat?"

"I think at first it was the medication, but she just quit eating. Sometimes it took me all day to feed her breakfast. We took it one bite at a time," he paused for a moment and stared into the field. Then he said, "And then there were her glasses. Oh I went through a time with her over her spectacles. She used to fight me. I'd worry with them, making sure she

86

had them during the day, but when I'd try to take them off of her at night she'd fight me and say, 'they're mine . . . mine, and you can't have 'em.' Eventually I reckoned it didn't matter one way or the other."

"I bet she was strong," I said recalling how strong Alzheimer's patients can be.

"Oh yeah, she might only have weighed seventy-nine pounds but she was strong. And she didn't want me or anyone else touching her stuff," he said as he smiled at the painful memory.

"I carried Marge home. I got her a hospital bed. I told the girls I was going to keep their mother at home. It just didn't make sense to send her to a nursing home," Billy said.

I imagine he'd applied the simple philosophy of treating Marge how he would want to be treated.

"I thought putting her in a home would make things worse for both of us. She'd be in a strange place. She might get scared, and I'd have to travel each day just to see her. Soon hospice started coming. I'd been getting her up to go to the bathroom and shower, but before too long she needed more help. The hospice girls bathed her in the bed, and the nurses came often. It seemed like someone was here every day. They were just like family. Marge stayed at home with me until she died," he said.

I knew that anything I said would be the wrong, but compassion demanded something be spoken.

"Billy, see these worry lines on my forehead?" I said while pointing to my face. "Did you notice during the years you cared for Marge that Alzheimer's erased the worry from her life?"

He thought for a moment. Slowly, a smile formed on his face and he answered, "You know, you're right. She used to fret about things a lot."

"Billy, just imagine. Even though she might have been unable to remember the ingredients she needed to make a cake, or where her glasses were, she also couldn't remember things that troubled her. Unlike the rest of us who worry about tomorrow, or our past mistakes, Marge lived from one moment to the next. She remembered the most important thing. She remembered you, and that you loved her. What could have been more important than that?" I asked.

His smile broadened.

I held my tears until I got in the car. The love he felt for his wife was evident in his care for her then, and in the simple gold band he still wears today. He treated his beloved wife with respect and compassion until her last breath. I could only imagine how difficult the past ten years had been and how lonely each day since her death has been. I pray that my last moments on this earth will be filled with as much love.

Chapter Fourteen

Breaking New Ground

"Momma always cleaned out the barn before planting the garden."
—Billy Albertson

Spring fever comes early for farmers like Billy. The first frost of fall is welcomed, because it signals the official end of the busy summer season and the beginning of a time to rest. Crops are gone and the cool night air provides the perfect weather for a slower pace and recuperative sleep. However, after about three nights of below freezing temperatures we were refreshed and itching with cabin fever.

"Would you lookie here," he said as he opened the front door for me to enter. "You've found some high water britches."

He was referring to my new overalls. Articles of clothing that are "high water" mean the cuff strikes above the ankle. Should one encounter a creek and need to cross, she could do so without getting wet. Kind of like Michael Jackson's slacks, only a lot less sparkly.

I looked down at my garb. While some believe overalls were designed for comfort, the lack of waistband left me feeling like I was mooning people as I walked. I kept checking the sides to make certain all three buttons were clasped. The style I wore was designed with a cuff at the knee, but since I'm vertically challenged, the cuffs hit me at the ankle. I had stenciled flowers on the pockets to glam things up a bit. A girl should do her best to look good, even in the garden. With the added decorations, my black shoes, white socks, and whiter legs I did look just a bit ridiculous.

"I figured if I was going to be a farmer, I needed to dress the part," I said.

"Where'd you find those?" Billy asked.

I smiled and twirled around. "I got them where smart folk shop, the Goodwill. Aren't you proud?"

Billy beamed and said, "Law, I love that place. I find stuff there all the time." Without warning he changed the subject and continued, "I've been thinking about next year's garden. Let me show you what I'm a planning."

We donned our jackets and stepped outside. Uncomfortable in the cool temperature, I plunged my hands in my pocket as Billy lead me into the garden.

"I think this year I'm going to plant cucumbers along this fence," he said gesturing toward a patch of grass near the grape vines. He turned to an area directly behind the house, "and of course I'll put the beans here, maybe add some beets . . . you like beets?"

Beets aren't exactly my favorite vegetable but I nodded because I knew he loved them. "I think there's going to be a need for your vegetables this year," I said, then added, "I don't think Jamie has much faith in me. She wants to grow a garden over here with you."

He nodded and looked toward a barrier fence which separates his property from the neighbor's. "I think I'll just let her have that spot right there then. I've got some old landscape timbers, we'll use them to mark her off a spot," he said.

I mistakenly thought this was a planning session, but while I surveyed Jamie's garden area he plunked a timber at my feet.

"Let me go get the tiller. See if you can find a shovel," he instructed.

In addition to a real tractor, he also owns a garden tiller. He cranked it at the shed and steered toward me, carefully walking the metal tines across the yard so as not to disturb the sparse grass. We dug a trench and laid the timbers. Then he re-cranked the tiller and used it to cut up the grass that was growing where Jamie's garden would be. I raked the area clean, filled the wheelbarrow, and tossed the uprooted grass into the chickens who were eager for something to scratch. Billy moved to the cucumber patch where I repeated the process while he made two passes with the tiller. I should have known I was in for trouble when he said, "Mother always made us clean out the chicken coop before breaking new ground."

He slipped into the shed, I assumed to retrieve the gas can. Wrong! He returned with a wheelbarrow full of chicken manure. Not the dry powdery kind one might assume; no it was wet, gooey, aromatic fowl excrement.

"I'm going to till this into the soil," he said. "That'll make everything grow real good."

Kind of makes one re-think organic vegetables, doesn't it? I kept my distance downwind as he incorporated the manure into the dirt.

"You can go get a load of wood chips if you want," he yelled above the whine of the motor.

It was my pleasure. I returned and shoveled chips behind Billy. He pressed down hard on the machine as the tines broke through clods of clay and blended the manure and mulch. Soon, all the organic matter was mixed into the soil. We stepped back, hands on hips and surveyed our work.

"Looks like we tore the ground up good," he said.

I nodded.

"You know beets and lettuce are winter crops," he said. "It's never too early to start them. I should probably till up the small garden too while you're here."

He hesitated for a moment and examined my tired expression. Then he said, "First, let's take a break."

We returned to the warmth of the house. In the winter, Billy keeps a fire burning in the wood-stove and uses a ceiling fan to distribute the heat. The result is a comforting warmth far better than what electric or gas provides. He stoked the fire and reached for a stack of pamphlets on top of the television. "I got us a Farmer's Almanac the other day," he said while placing a small newspaper print booklet in my hand. "Have a look and tell me if there is anything we can plant today."

I wanted to say, "Didn't we just harvest everything last week? How could it possibly be time to replant?" But I did as instructed. Remarkably, several crops could be planted, "when frost danger passes."

Billy believes that something, usually potatoes, must be planted on Good Friday. I'm not sure if there is any biblical significance to this tradition, but my dad adheres to the same unwritten rule. In fact, Dad plants his entire garden on Good Friday, despite uncertain weather patterns and the statistical probability of frost. According to the *203rd Annual Issue of Grier's Almanac*, the stars and signs were properly aligned permitting the continuation of the potato planting. Time to get out the tiller, again.

Each year my mother gives me a N.C. Clampitt Hardware calendar. This is her tool for interpreting the zodiac, what some people call "the signs." The ability to know which phase the moon is in is an all important gift passed down from generation to generation. Mother has tried to explain the signs to me, but I just can't seem to sift through the convoluted information and apply it to farming.

When I was scheduled to have my surgery mother insisted I postpone the procedure until the signs changed. "The signs are in the secrets," she whispered gravely. "You never, ever want to have surgery when the signs are in the secrets."

I reasoned that since the surgery was in my secret place, I'd be fine.

Mother never cans vegetables when the signs are in the secrets or the bowels. I seem to recall she doesn't can when they are in the feet either. She plants corn when the signs are in the neck, so "the stalks will grow as high as your head."

I plant when Billy tells me to.

For those who have never glanced inside the cover of an almanac it is chocked full of helpful information. The garden calendar lists specific dates that are the best time for planting root crops, which, when I cross referenced with the dates on the Clampitt Hardware calendar, discovered the signs are in the feet and knees. Above ground crops should be planted when the signs are in the arms and head. The logic behind Mother's planting notion was beginning to take shape, especially when I reviewed the section marked, "plant killing." Several days each month are set aside for the eradication of unwanted plants. Since I have an abundance of English Ivy, I decided to read further. According to Grier's, the killing signs are the heart, bowels, and legs. This made perfect sense. I hate ivy with all my heart. My legs could stomp the vines, and once I pulled them up . . . well, the rest can be figured out.

Nestled between the pages of the publication I also found a fishing calendar and tonics for sale that will cure every ailment imaginable. But perhaps the most surprising discovery was The Ten Commandments. Churches used to mandate the memorization of God's rules during Sunday school classes. Unfortunately, I fear those days may be gone. I'm embarrassed to say that I no longer can recite all ten from memory. Billy probably can.

One of the commandments he will not break under any circumstance applies to the Sabbath (Sunday). Using the Douay version of the Bible, published in 1609, the almanac reads: "Six days shall thou labour, and do all thy work. But the seventh day *is* the Sabbath of the Lord thy God; in it thou shalt not do any work."

There are no vegetables available at the farm on Sunday. No goats or chickens for sale either. He does not exchange money, or pick vegetables regardless of how ripe, on the Sabbath. Sunday is God's day. Maybe it's just me, but I find comfort in that philosophy.

I can still recall when Sunday was devoted to God and family. Few stores were open, and those that did business opened at 1pm to allow their workers time for church. The entire family went to church, together. Afterward, they ate lunch then visited family, friends, or folk in the nursing home. In the absence of visiting, they took a freshly washed car for a drive. Sunday *was* a day of rest. A day of recuperation from the exhausting work-week that had just been completed. It was a day to soak in some scripture, enjoy family and regroup for the week ahead. But now, unfortunately, Sunday is just another ordinary day to fill with obligations.

"Zippy, take one of those wheelbarrows and bring me a load of manure," Billy yelled across the bare garden.

One would think we had exhausted the supply of manure; but I promise the amount goats produce is inexhaustible.

While Billy knows everything there is to know about above ground vegetables, I know a thing or two about planting potatoes. Despite what will be protests from "real farmers," I can attest that any kind of potato will grow, even the store bought ones that sprout beneath the kitchen sink. No, they won't produce a harvest like those grown from certified seed. They may be small and imperfect, but if a potato is discovered putting forth white shoots in search of the sun, plant those babies and see what happens.

In order to properly grow white or "Irish" potatoes, first cut them into sections which contains a bud, also known as an "eye." Tender shoots emerge from the eye and ultimately turn into green leafy vines. Once a potato is sliced it is referred to as "seed."

Billy placed his open pocketknife in my hand and said, "Here, cut up the taters and I'll lay off the rows . . . careful, it's sharp."

I didn't need the warning. Even his butter knife is sharp.

I've been taught that once seeds are cut it is wise to let them "scab over," meaning allow the slices to become partially dry before planting. The reasoning behind the wives' tale is that a lower moisture level translates into a healthier plant. Billy had obviously never heard about this because the rows were ready before I had finished my part.

Gardeners are instructed to cover potato seeds with three to five inches of soil. Billy and I don't believe in covering anything that deep.

We think it takes the plant longer to emerge from the ground. Ideally, we want to drop a chunk of tater in the ground and see green leaves the following day. Yes, I realize potatoes are grown in rows that are mounded with several inches of dirt. Eventually our patch will look that way. Once leaves appear then we'll rake more dirt around them. Later we'll add a layer of mulch and more dirt. But for now, they are lightly covered with a mixture of soil, mulch and manure.

Hundreds of miles from Georgia, my dad was bent over his own little piece of ground; his work, a mirror of ours. There's comfort in that; in the way Mother Nature binds us together, easing our pain as we work the soil. The feel of dirt on our fingers lets us know that everything will somehow turn out fine. Since I knew he'd worked hard today I thought I'd call to check on him.

"What did you do today?" I asked, then quickly added, "bet you took the day off."

"Aw, nothing much. Just planted a few hills of taters," he answered.

"Me too. I planted an entire bag," I said implying that I'd planted a 50 pound bag instead of the two pound bag that had sprouted in the basement.

For Dad a "few hills" meant he *had* planted a fifty pound bag. He planted six rows of potatoes: two at his house, four at his mother's. I don't know how he finds the time, or the strength between working and worrying about Mother, but he managed to get everything in the ground before the sun set on another Good Friday.

Chapter Fifteen

A Replacement Grandpa

"A good man is hard to find."
—Renea Winchester

I was answering the question, "What are your summer plans?" by explaining my gardening friendship with Billy when Mother interrupted and said, "Renea's found a replacement grandpa."

I was stunned.

Frank Winchester was my one and only grandpa. My mother's dad, Lawson Styles, died of a heart attack when she was nineteen-years-old. Like most families, mine's seen heartache. Shortly after Lawson died, my dad's brother, Lawrence, was killed by a drunk driver a few days before Christmas. I've been told Frank wept for months and was never the same. But through death, springs life and ten months after Lawrence was buried a beautiful baby girl was born.

I am that girl.

Babies heal hearts and dry tears. Bittersweet, never ending, unconditional love was given to me. And though I admit I was spoiled, it wasn't in the way most would imagine. Gifts of toys and ponies weren't lavished upon me. I wasn't prone to tantrums and fits of rage when I didn't get my way. Instead, love, that all-healing gift, surrounded me. When I visited my grandparents the room exploded in laughter. Their faces lit up, hands clapped, arms opened, wrapped around me then squeezed. The more love they gave, the more I gave in return.

We Winchesters are a joyful lot, and it seemed, though I had no way of knowing, my birth had healed Frank's broken heart. I was the first grandchild and the only granddaughter for more than a decade. There are many people who can't understand the bond we shared, and even today it's difficult to explain.

I can't speak for him, although five years ago while we were sitting in church he patted my hand and spoke in a loud voice saying, "You know you always were my favorite." I curled my hand inside his, scooted closer, and squeezed him tight. I collected the words from his lips and pressed them deep inside my heart. Grandma, who never sat beside him because he refused to wear a hearing aid, and was prone to wind his watch if the preacher went past twelve o'clock, turned around and gave him "the look."

As long as he was in my world, I knew someone loved me unconditionally. By that I mean he loved me for who I was, not what I did for him. Most of us crave this kind of love: Pure love without conditions, love that is earned by being, living, loving. This type of love says, "I'll love you regardless. I'll love you because you're part of me. I'll love you because being around you makes me feel special."

Grandpa was the moral compass and boundary setter for me, more so than my parents. He often said, "It don't matter what you become when you grow up, just be somebody." The more he loved me, the harder I worked to make him proud.

The day he was taken I wish it had been me.

There was no warning. Sure, he was "getting on in years," but we had an agreement. I'd let him know when I could handle his death, and then he could go.

But God didn't ask for my permission.

It was a day like any other. The children were running late which meant I was also behind schedule.

"There's a bird in the garage," my son said.

A bird in the garage stopped me cold. A bird inside could only mean one thing . . . death. I shook the rural Appalachian superstition from my thoughts, took the children to school and returned home to gather my things for work. I was walking into the house when the phone rang.

Mother didn't even say hello. "Jesus came and took Grandpa this morning," she said the moment the receiver touched my ear. Her words were heavy and final.

"No," I said. "No Momma. Anyone . . . anyone, but him."

And though I know I should have been glad that God took him quick, I can promise I was not.

As wonderful as Billy Albertson is, he is no Frank Winchester. Yes, they share similar traits. Billy tests a knife's sharpness on his arm. Grandpa, immodest and proud of his pasty pale legs, tested his on bony shins. Both have compassion for others, giving without asking for anything in return. In the short time I've known Billy, he'd extended the hand of friendship to all. He'd been generous toward everyone he'd met. He welcomes me with a smile that says, "Come. Stay. I'm glad you're here."

Billy treats me like family.

Similarly, my Grandpa was a father figure to many children in the community. He offered store credit at Winchester's Grocery, a country store he ran that paralleled a busy two-lane road in rural western North Carolina. The store was compact with a cold cement floor and pot-belly stove that served as a gathering spot for the Friday night banjo pickers. Rickety wood shelves, thick with road dust held everything one needed: groceries, penny candy, cigarettes, and over the counter medication. Grandpa built a room where he stored a variety of animal feed. And of course there were "dopes in a bottle," otherwise known as Coca-Cola. Even with a shelf of candy to choose from it was the wheel cheese I craved. It was displayed beside the cash register alongside the carving knife. While most folk bought their cheese by the pound, Grandpa would painstakingly slice piece upon piece of paper thin cheese into my outstretched hand.

Oh, to taste a slice of wheel cheese again.

Many families had a credit account at the store. With unemployment always in the double digits in my hometown, credit was the only way most people could feed their families. Grandpa knew some folk would never pay. Yet he allowed them to run up a high balance because "it's not the children's fault their dad can't find work." He was a good man, and those are hard to find. When Grandpa closed the store thousands of dollars were still owed him.

After Jesus took him home, the grapevine rustled with the news that Frank Winchester had died. Casseroles were delivered to my grandma; then, in the ultimate sign of respect, the men of the community dug his grave using only hand tools. The night his body lay in the funeral home, a line of mourners stretched around the building and the sheriff's department dispatched deputies for traffic control.

While Billy works until he collapses and takes care of his tools, Grandpa was a cobbler. He half-way did things, opting to wait until the last possible moment, like after something collapsed into pieces, before attempting maintenance.

Grandpa smoked. Unfiltered camel cigarettes seemed permanently wedged between his gigantic fingertips. He smoked in every room of the house, but it was in the bathroom where he got in trouble. No matter how many times Grandma forbade him to smoke in the bathroom, every morning he'd light a cigarette and take a few puffs while shaving. He'd place the smoldering nubs on the edge of the sink and ignore the glowing tip that inched closer toward the counter. Finally, all that remained was powdery ash inside charred groves of the Formica.

"One of these days he's going to burn the house down," Grandma complained.

Billy wouldn't smoke a cigarette on a dare.

Billy has one dirty joke and it goes like this:

"You know how to speak mule?" he asks.

Most shake their head no.

Then he continues, "Well, a mule's brain can only hold two or three words, like gee. That means turn right, and haw for turn left. Then of course there's whoa which means stop. When I was growing up we had two mules named Gee and Key. Once I was driving 'em mules plowing up the garden. Old Key got out of control and wouldn't turn left and I was a yellin' Haw . . . Key . . . Haw . . . Key."

In contrast, Grandpa was the community joker. The father of five children, he often told the story of learning there was about to be another baby added to the family.

Grandpa joked, "Yup, I learned I'za gonna be the dad of a half dozen young'uns and the news was more than I could bear. I went out to the barn and threw a rope over the rafters. I fastened the rope good and tight around my neck and clumb up on an apple box. I was about to jump off when the thought occurred to me that I might be hanging an innocent man."

Grandma didn't like that joke too much.

Once, my parents and I were at the store getting our weekly Moon Pie and "dopes in a bottle" when Grandpa came running out to the car.

He said, "Son, I need you to get a look at my new mouse trap. You know how the rats have been eating up my feed profit. Well, I've gone and got me a bone-a-fide ball-bearing rat trap. This feller gave it to me for free and guaranteed it'd take care of my rat problem." Deep laugh lines creased his face as he spoke. "I've only had it a couple of hours and already it's caught four rats."

Dad stepped into the feed room, eager to get a look at new fangled contraption. Grandpa busied himself waiting on a customer and tried not to laugh.

Dad returned from the feed room shrugging his shoulders and said, "You're gonna have to come show it to me, I can't find it nowhere."

Grandpa entered the room and pointed to a well-endowed yellow tomcat and laughed.

Mother directed my brother and I into the car. I was too young to understand the joke then, but I often think of the punchline and smile.

While Billy and Grandpa share common traits, no one has ever bent on one knee and engulfed me in arms that sheltered me from the world. Grandpa did when I was a toddler, and never stopped reaching for me even after I turned forty and his knees creaked in protest.

That kind of love can never be replaced. Why would I ever try?

Chapter Sixteen

Building Fences Out of Duck Feet

"It takes a strong fence to keep a goat outta trouble."
—Billy Albertson

The time had come to wean the kids from their mothers. This is a painful process for all children, whether human or goat. I stood with Billy and watched, both of us smiling, as the kids frolicked and played, jumping and twisting in mid-air.

"Those little critters feel so good they can barely keep their feet on the ground," he said.

It was true. Like Tigger in *Winnie-The-Pooh*, the kids bounced, jumped and climbed their way into trouble while under the watchful eyes of their mothers.

"I want you to look over there," he said, pointing to the woodshed.

I turned to find several critters circling his neatly stacked wood pile. They curiously sniffed and nibbled on the bark. In a mischievous game of follow the leader, the largest goat, who we'd named Sampson, climbed the stack. Of course, his playmates followed. Sampson arrived at the top and looked down as if challenging his playmates to knock him off.

"Looks like they're playing King-Of-The-Mountain," Billy commented.

Suddenly the wood shifted, and the goats tumbled to the ground. They rushed to the safety of their mother, each looking at the other as if to say, "I didn't do it." After a quick drink of milk, curiosity got the best of them and they returned to sniff the wood.

Billy looked at the critters and said, "I'm thinking about building a fence to separate the kids from the nannies."

This was his way of asking for my help. It's a mistake to stop at Billy's when I'm in a hurry. Since the weather was chilly and the forecast predicted rain, I'd brought homemade vegetable soup for lunch and planned on staying a while. Jamie was out of school and wanted to check on Kelly, the newest kid, who had just turned two weeks old.

"Let me put the soup on the stove, then we can get to work," I said.

Billy took me to the corner of the fence where the Normandy chickens are currently residing. He'd separated this exotic pair of poultry with plumage on their head from the common chickens hoping the hen would hatch some "fancy chicks."

"I reckon if I drill me a post in the ground here," he said while pointing, "then connect it to that support post on yon side I can make me a good lot."

I nodded and said, "Looks like it'll work."

"I have a gate in the barn and enough fencing to string me a line from this corner to the other. Then when it comes time to wean the kids, I'll take them away from their mothers and put 'em in here," he said.

There is something endearing about the way he calls the nanny goats mothers. This precious man treats every animal on his farm with kindness. Weeks earlier, I had decided if I was going to be an unpaid farm hand at Billy's plantation I needed a place to store my essentials. Real gardeners, like I hoped one day to become, need certain necessities like new gloves and a sun visor. I had found an empty nail in the shed and hung my accessories, noting at the time how ridiculous and out of place my items looked beside the rusty tools and unpainted weathered siding. My adornments practically screamed, "City girl playing sharecropper."

I donned my unstained gloves and zipped my jacket, then followed him to a place in the field where a bulky section of chain-link fence had been lying on the ground so long the weeds formed a pattern in the grass. Billy grabbed a section of fencing, and tugged. Eager to help, I went to the other end and bent down.

"Let me get this," he said. "It's all marred up. No telling which-a-way it'll come when I pull."

Having no experience with fence building, I obeyed.

Once the grass gave up the fence, it became an unruly, accordion-like slinky. Billy pulled it toward the construction site. He allowed me to assist only after the goats tried to help.

"Looks like Daisy's gonna be the foreman," I said after Daisy, the white goat with a purple collar and tiny bell around her neck, decided to jump on top of the fence as it was being dragged.

"Oh yeah. Goats are curious creatures," Billy announced.

While I'm no builder, I love creating things. I wish I were a woman who could read a blueprint and operate a saw. I'd love to have a tree house on my property. My husband refused to teach me how to operate any type of machinery after I failed to properly secure a ladder and almost broke my fool neck while painting the foyer. Instead, I bake.

In the fantasy land of television cooking shows, ingredients are pre-measured. Utensils stand polished and ready. The chef, never looking at a recipe, tosses in a bit of this and a pinch of that and presto . . . dinner. Inside this bubble of culinary creativity, one might imagine this is how cooking is actually done, in a spotless kitchen with perfectly measured ingredients and no cleanup. In reality, my kitchen is chaotic at best with messes on the marble, flour on the floor and a mustard stain on the ceiling the result of shaking the bottle without first checking the lid. My husband observes that I have the knack of using every pot, pan, and bowl while making one simple dish. I like to think of it as a gift.

In this way, Billy and I are twins. Fence building with Billy is much like baking with me. If I have not used every tool in the shed and am not dirty from head to toe, then I have not had fun. Of course it's best to gather all tools, materials, and building implements prior to breaking ground. But what kind of fun am I having if I don't have to stop and chase a goat who has decided to carry off the hammer the moment I turned my back?

Even though I have six measuring cups in my kitchen, I can never find one when I need it. Billy owns four shovels. In theory there should be one placed in each corner of the property with one in the barn, shed, garage, and a fourth near the tractor. But alas, like measuring cups there is never a shovel around when I am ready to dig.

Billy gave up the shovel search and returned with a post hole digger. While I understand the concept behind this contraption, it seemed a post hole digger wastes time and effort. Billy raised the tool high above his head then slammed it into the compacted clay. The dull mouth thudded into the earth, leaving two half-moon marks in the grass. He moved the handles. The metal mouth pinched closed capturing a tiny amount of dirt inside. He turned and jiggled the handles until the mouth opened and spat dirt into a pile at his feet. He repeated this process until he had created an adequate hole. All while Daisy stepped daintily between the links of the fence, sniffing each section making sure our work was acceptable.

With the hole dug, Billy mixed concrete and installed the fence post. During this time I watched as he measured, went back to the shed and returned with a bucket of bent nails and three iron stakes.

"Now what I'm going do here," Billy said, "is drive these support beams into the ground at a 45-degree angle. That way when I string the wire it won't sag. I'll have a good strong fence."

Were I a man, I suppose this would be the time to offer my suggestions. Or perhaps adjust myself, pause to spit, and pontificate about my fence building prowess. Instead I nodded and said, "Yup. Sounds like a plan."

Billy dropped his burden with a clatter. "Cause it takes a good strong fence to keep goats outta trouble. Now I need to retrieve some duck-feet," he said.

I asked myself, *what in the world are duck feet other than the obvious appendages ducks need to travel from one place to the next?*

He returned with three v-shaped metal blades.

"These here things are duck-feet cultivators," he explained.

I had noticed the blades hanging from the beams of the shed. "I thought they were part of a tractor," I said.

"Oh yeah. They're parts of an old tiller." He held out a blade for me to examine. "They don't turn the dirt like regular blades. They work more like a hoe, lightly breaking up the ground. These here are worn out, so I'll use them as a scotch," Billy explained.

While his idea was a brilliant way to reuse the blades, I thought the heavy pieces of rusty metal still looked usable. But then again, what could I possibly know about duck feet? I cringed as the beautiful antique blades sank into the earth beneath the weight of a ten-pound hammer. I was going to miss the feet dangling from the rafters, welcoming me as I walked under their rusty shape. Maybe it's the pack-rat in me that wanted to keep the blades in the shed. They had decorated the structure giving it character, hanging on bent antiquated nails symbolizing Billy's life as a sharecropper. Now buried, they were gone forever.

With the necessary tools and implements finally located, it was time to hammer everything into place then stretch the wire. Billy positioned the metal support beam at a forty five degree angle then asked me to hold it while he straightened the nails.

"I hardly ever buy nails," he said while placing one on top of the wooden fencepost and tapping it into submission. "I just straighten these here crooked ones out and use them again."

I made a mental note to buy a box of nails for his birthday.

Billy commenced banging the nail into the wooden post. When the head was almost flush with the post he turned the hammer and used the claw part to bend the nail sideways in what I could only assume was a method of securing them in place for all eternity. He then pounded the bent portion into the wood for good measure. Many people call this technique "cobbled up." And while the supplies he used weren't shiny and new, and the end result not the quality seen on Home and Garden Television, his work was both functional and adequate.

By now two hours had elapsed. Fifteen nails had been straightened, three antiquated duck-feet buried, and two support posts hammered into place with just-straightened, now re-bent-at-the-neck nails.

Billy pulled on his jacket and announced, "It's time for a break."

This was one of only a few times he had stopped working before a project was finished. I noticed he was sniffling a bit. He seemed to be catching a cold. I worry about him and how hard he pushes himself.

Before we ate. Billy prayed, "Our Father, as we bow Lord we want to thank you for another day. Thank you for waking us up this morning. We want to thank you for our health and for the nourishment you have set before us. Bless Zippy's family Lord, and bless this food for the nourishment of our bodies and our bodies to your kingdom. Amen."

It's not pity that keeps me coming to Billy's, or the fresh vegetables. Although the thought of him eating alone everyday is heartbreaking; I get lonely too. Maybe it's the transient nature of the city that keeps me from developing what I feel are deep, long-lasting friendships. I want a friend I can do fun things with. Not shop, or get my nails done, but someone to spend time with, who encourages me to be a better person. While most people laugh when I tell them about my friendship with Billy, I can say with all sincerity that he may be the only real friend I have in Atlanta.

Admittedly, I do look for excuses to visit him. I carry chicken scraps, plastic bags, and empty jars, things I know he can use. Not new things; he wants to pay me for anything new I bring. And today, as I stood holding an oxidized metal support beam while he hammered, I knew my help wasn't worth much, but maybe it would be enough to keep him from spending all day alone outside in the cold, even though I needed the companionship more than he.

I was surprised when I returned to our work site and discovered the goats had overturned the nails and scattered them all over the pasture. Billy acted like this was an everyday occurrence. He was happy he'd remembered that a shovel was in back of the truck, and quickly dug a shallow trench for the fence tines.

"If I bury the fence, it'll keep varmints out," he explained.

He picked up the slinky-fence and positioned it against the gate. "Here," he said. "Hold this while I go get my come-hither." I stretched my arms as wide as possible. The unwieldy chains threatened to roll up like a tongue and swallow me. My shoulders cramped and my arms shook all while I wondered, *what in the world is a come-hither?*

Billy returned with a rust-covered winch. He fumbled to unlatch the cable while I ignored cramps forming between my shoulder blades. I began to pray I wouldn't topple backward.

"I think I need to pull some of the kinks out of the fence before we nail it up," he said. "Go ahead and lay it down."

I was happy to oblige. I picked up the goat-strewn nails while Billy placed a landscape timber beneath the kinked links. The perfect nail-straightening tool was propped against a post. I reached for the ten-pound hammer, dragging it as I walked. Now all I had to do was hold the nail by the head, watch that I didn't mash my finger, and bang it with the bulky hammer. One minute it's crooked, the next straight.

"This is where the tree fell on the fence," he said while stomping on a bent link. "I think I can straighten it out." He reached toward me. "Zippy, hand me the persuader."

First a "come-hither," now a "persuader." I looked around hoping to find something marked "persuader" lying on the ground.

"You're holding it," he said.

Billy took the ten-pound-persuader-hammer and quickly aligned the links while I straightened more nails with the claw hammer. He placed the tines in the trench and aligned the fence to the wooden post while I fed him a steady stream of straightened nails. He pounded everything in place.

"Now. Let me go get the truck and pull the fence tight," Billy said.

It was around this time I began to get concerned about our little project. As I mentioned earlier, I'm no builder, but even I know using a truck to tighten a fence is a tad bit dangerous. But because this sounded exactly like something I'd do I said, "Oh Boy, let's go."

I held the gate open while the truck sputtered inside. I ran to the second gate and laughed as the goats fled in every direction, putting distance between them and the vehicle. This day was becoming more exciting than a visit to the circus.

With one end of the fence secured, he hooked the come-hither to yon end of the fence, the other to the trunk's bumper, then cranked the handle.

I stood amazed, while the gears groaned, and pulled, and stretched the fence.

Billy tested the fence by leaning against it. He unlocked the come-hither and announced, "Almost done." He hopped into the truck, gave her a crank then pulled the truck forward, all without a word of warning.

Before I could gather my senses and move to safety he was done.

"Now, that's better," he said with a nod. "Hand me some more nails."

I turned to find Daisy standing beside the bucket. A leather glove with duct tape covering the fingers was sticking out of her mouth.

"That's a goat for ya," Billy said while I rescued his glove, "always in the way."

Two more hours passed as we completed the project. Then we piled the nails, come- hither, persuader, and other implements into the back of the truck.

With one hand on the key, the other on the steering wheel he announced, "Stand clear and get ready for a rodeo."

I rushed to open the gate. Instead of pulling the truck forward, he did a donut in the field like a teenager driving a hot-rod. The truck bounced and jostled as he ran over the feed trough. A small piece of lumber wedged beneath the bumper making a thumping sound as he approached. Goats scattered and I tried not to wet my pants as a real live goat rodeo, more entertaining than Ringling Brothers, played out before my eyes. Behind me the rooster sounded an alarm, or possibly a cheer.

As I closed the gate Daisy was rubbing her body against the newly installed fence and checking out our handiwork. I think she approved.

Chapter Seventeen

Naughty Dog

"Ain't Nothing We Can Do About It, A Dog Will be A Dog."
—Billy Albertson

Gypsy crouched and looked toward the driveway. The car was gone. The coast was clear. She lunged forward and began digging. The metal tag bearing her name jingled as dirt flew backward from between her hind-feet.

The sound of claws scratching against the chain-linked fence alerted the chickens of danger. They stood still, heads-cocked toward the disturbance. The hens clucked a low, "guurl," causing the rooster to strut over and investigate. Seeing no intruder, he crowed a precautionary warning then clucked an "all clear" for his hens to resume scratching. Dipstick watched nervously from the protection of his bed. He growled at Gypsy who turned toward her brother and pondered the warning for a split second before returning to work. *Fine*, Dipstick thought. *Don't say I didn't warn you.* He turned around twice and settled down on his bed with a thump. Trouble was coming and he wanted no part of it.

Dipstick and Gypsy are black and white Mountain Feist dogs. It is believed the breed originated in North America several hundred years ago a cross between English Terriers and the American Indian wild dog. At first glance, most folk mistake Feists for Jack Russell Terriers. Both are balls of energy wrapped inside a petite and loveable canine body. If anyone has the time and patience to train these eager animals, he'll have a devoted companion for life.

Most farmers struggle to control rats that come out at night and eat their fill of feed while leaving their droppings behind. Farmers use cats and dogs to control these disease carrying vermin. Feists, who love to hunt rats, are the perfect choice of rodent control. They also serve as a burglar alarm, barking a fierce warning to those who approach their territory, which is why Billy placed them near the chicken coop, to protect the flock.

These swift, agile dogs were also bred to hunt rabbits, squirrels, and other small game like helpless, defenseless, free range chickens.

Sometimes he is just too trusting.

I imagine Gypsy waited patiently until she heard Billy's car leave the driveway. Billy, on his way to church, had no inkling of her plan. I picture Gypsy licking the saliva forming in her mouth, clicking her teeth in anticipation, excited to the point of pacing.

I keep telling myself, she just couldn't control herself.

I'm certain Dipstick wanted no part of the trouble that was coming. But Gypsy, she ignored her brother's warning, then tunneled into the chicken house and slaughtered her master's chickens.

Hours later, Billy returned from church to find a small tunnel into the coop and twenty hens dead inside. Dipstick was in his bed wearing the *I-told-you-so* look and Gypsy, well, she couldn't deny her guilt considering she was found with a dead chicken in her mouth.

As luck would have it, I arrived shortly after the massacre. While I cried at the loss of the chickens I'd been feeding and the senseless killing, Billy's response was, "I reckon I had too many hens anyway."

He buried the poultry and continued with the chores of the day reminding me that, "There ain't nothing we can do about it Gypsy was just being a dog."

All farmers know that once a dog develops the "taste for blood" it's nearly impossible to squelch their desire. Farmers who depend on the sale of livestock for their livelihood have been known to "put down" a dog who kills for sport. I've also heard stories of shocking collars being used; some have even tried tying a dead chicken around the dog's neck to "break them from the taste for blood."

Billy would never do something like that.

While I cried, he explained, "It's their nature, no way to change them."

The Feist puppies arrived on the farm years ago despite protests from his daughters. They believed two puppies were the last thing Billy needed. Marge's health was deteriorating and (they thought) he didn't need the added responsibility.

But daughters don't always know best. They would soon discover that Dipstick and Gypsy were exactly what Billy needed. That winter was filled with life-challenges for Billy. He was struggling to care for Marge. whose health was declining. And as often happens, just when one thinks he can't handle anything else, circumstances change for the worst. Before the winter was over, Billy had buried four siblings.

The puppies soon outgrew their house. Billy had determined they would be outside dogs. Companions who would keep him company in the field ... outside dogs for an outside man. They followed Billy everywhere, looking up at him for guidance and direction. Perhaps Billy imagined they'd keep the goats in line, though I doubt it. Goats, like cats can be stubborn.

Billy fashioned a doghouse from a non-working washing machine. He gutted the appliance, and then installed thick layers of insulation followed by sheets of cloth to regulate the temperature. Of course he made certain there was no risk the door would close and trap them inside. He transformed the washer into a Kenmore condo, and the dogs seemed pleased. His grandson, Matthew, helped him construct a fence which was used more for safety than to keep them confined. With so many cars entering Billy's driveway during the summer, the dogs needed a safe place to stay during the day.

Dipstick and Gypsy were promoted to garden supervisors. Billy clipped their chain to a clothesline that paralleled the property then set out to get the daily chores done. The dogs watched, I suspect, fascinated that anyone would enjoy working in the sun. Billy was no stranger to the heat, but the dogs, well, they needed a place beneath the shade of a pecan tree, albeit attached to a clothesline. They guarded their master, kept an eye on the goats, and let Billy know when customers arrived by barking a welcome.

At the end of the day, when he thought no one was looking, Billy unhooked them and let the pups run. Like a child, he chased his Mountain Feists around the field, all three scampering as they ran around the pecan tree. Of course he's forgiven Gypsy for killing the hens. Even now, in the cool of the evening, he plays with Dipstick and Gypsy in his back yard revealing a carefree child-like spirit I suspect most folk wish they had.

Chapter Eighteen

Timber!

"Santa, All I Really Want for Christmas is a Chainsaw."
—Renea Winchester

Everywhere I looked something around my house needed work. Grand plans formed in my mind as I sketched and planned a vegetable garden, greenhouse, goat house, chicken house, and even an outside storage shed in which to keep my tools. I envisioned a rock pathway meandering through the woods. It would lead to a pond or maybe a brook that gurgled and babbled filling the property with peaceful sounds. There was only one problem with my design, trees. In order to convert the property into the perfect plot of serenity I'd need to kill a few dozen trees.

At my house killing helpless trees is a serious matter. Several years back when the pine beetle devastated eighty trees in our yard, my husband and I walked the property wringing our hands trying to postpone the inevitable. We knew the trees must be removed. We called several "tree services" (read tree killers) to survey the situation and suggest how best to remove the dead pines. The problem was the large number of mature, glorious dogwoods scattered throughout the property. We didn't want any healthy trees harmed and certainly not a dogwood.

"We'll use every precaution to avoid the dogwoods," Captain Tree Killer assured us. He presented us with a can of orange paint and said, "Spray the trees you want us to avoid with this, and they'll be safe." Then he left.

Then the massacre began.

Because I naively believed professional crews still removed trees like my dad did, meaning cut each one down with a saw, then slice it into manageable, removable sections, I was shocked when I noticed a bobcat scraping a road through my front yard. Following closely behind was another piece of machinery called a cherry picker. There weren't any chainsaws, only heavy equipment raping the forest in front of my house.

I have yet to understand why most workers think I'm a ditzy woman with only two brain cells that barely rub together. Yes I realize (now) that I should have clearly asked, "You men do know how to operate a chainsaw . . . right?" before allowing them free reign on my property with massive tree-killing death machines.

The sound of pines slapping into each other and the hum of the wood chipper was deafening. I stood frozen as the bobcat bumped into a tree that had been clearly marked off limits with orange paint. As delicate white flowers fell to the earth, my mother's words resonated in my ears, "If you want something done right, do it yourself."

This was one of her many life mottos, and with this one I happen to agree. If I had a chainsaw I could have done a better job than these bozos. Granted, it would have taken me more than a year to cut down all the diseased pines, but still, my beloved Dogwoods would have been safe. I quickly called my husband who rushed home to handle the situation.

I couldn't wait. I tried to stop the workers, but no one spoke English.

I rummaged for Captain Tree Killer's business card and between hysterical tears told him he must come to my house immediately.

"Your workers are killing my trees and making a mess of the entire front yard."

By the time he reached the house every single Dogwood that had been marked with protective paint was nicked and bleeding sap.

Then my daughter stepped off the bus. It didn't help matters that she was learning about the environment in school, or that God had blessed her with red hair and a temper to match. While my husband was telling Captain Tree Killer, "You'd better fix this mess, real quick before the little lady gets a hold of you," he spied Jamie surveying the damage.

"Oh no," he said as she dropped her backpack and ran toward the disaster zone. "I think you and your crew need to take a break. I might be able to save you from the wife, but the red headed one is getting ready to ream you out."

Captain Tree Killer laughed.

"You got a wife?" Dennis asked.

The smile left Captain Tree Killer's face as he nodded.

114

"Do you have daughters?"

He nodded again.

"Then you understand what's about to happen if you don't leave," my husband explained.

He then spent the rest of the afternoon consoling us as we mourned the death of our precious trees.

While the number of hardwoods I needed removed for my personal oasis was small compared to the tree killing debacle, I had vowed I would never allow a professional tree company access to my property again. What I needed was someone with knowledge and the tools to get the job done. I mentioned my manual laborer need to Billy. He's the go-to man, the authority on all things livestock, garden, and forest thinning. I knew he wouldn't give me the name of just any old Joe Six Pack with a chainsaw and a pickup truck; he'd refer me to someone with real tree-dropping skill.

"What size are those trees you need shed of?" he asked.

"Well they're Poplar trees," I said, like the species would matter. "So they'll be easy to cut down. And, I've measured the area. I only need three dropped. The largest one is about four inches around. A man who knows what he's doing could bring them down in no time."

Billy was on my doorstep the next morning.

"I reckon today'd be as good as any to cut them trees down," he said.

I grabbed a jacket and we began.

"Let me have a look at what you need," he said while scanning the front yard. "Go shut my trunk and set out the gas and oil."

I did as told then followed him to the trees. I stood at the road supervising while he wielded the heavy chainsaw. He had designated a drop zone and forbade my entrance. I couldn't help but wonder what kind of woman asks a seventy-seven-year-old man to do this kind of work? I imagined those who passed said, "Just look at her working that old man half to death."

People do talk.

With skill I've only seen my dad match, Billy cut a small chunk of flesh from one side of the trunk, then positioned the saw on the other side and pressed hard on the gas. Smoke and dust filled the air as did the unmistakeable grinding sound of the engine groaning while it cut through pulpy flesh. In a few minutes the tree crashed to the ground.

"Stand clear while I cut these to stove length," Billy warned.

I obeyed.

Billy removed the smallest limbs first then made short work cutting the trunk into logs that would fit inside my fireplace. With a nod, he signaled when it was time for me to haul the wood to the house. I filled the wheelbarrow and pushed. By the time I returned, the first tree was cut into firewood and the second was down.

I paused long enough to remove a layer of clothing. There's something about working with Billy that causes one to sweat. By the time I had the first tree neatly stacked beside the house, he had dropped all three trees and was working on another he thought needed to go. I offered him a drink of water.

"I figure these little birches were in your way," he said while taking a seat on a stump. He turned the bottle up and took a drink. "That'll let a lot of sunshine in."

I've asked my husband, no, begged him, to buy me a chainsaw for my birthday. I've asked Santa also, but someone has told St. Nick I'm grounded from all motorized contraptions.

I'm the kind of gal who likes to get things done. If I want a room painted I grab the drop cloth and the paintbrush and start slapping paint on the wall. My husband has been supportive of my get-it-done side until I thought a tree house was in order. He's an engineer, so I assumed this would be a fun do-it-together project. I approached him with a suggestion, followed by a design plan. When a subtle hint didn't work, I realized I was on my own and picked up the Skil saw.

In hindsight, I should have used the downstairs entrance to the basement instead of trekking up and down the stairs. After the third trip past my husband, this time with operating instructions for the saw in hand, the "what-is-that-woman-up-to" alarm sounded in his brain.

I had measured the board and marked it with a thick carpenter's pencil. I flicked the chalk-line, a fun tool no *real* carpenter is without, and was ready to make the first cut. The saw was equipped with some kind of wife-proof safety design which required the operator to press a button with a pinky finger, wrap a cord around the thumb, lift a hand to the sky as if in prayer, and then squeeze the trigger.

I had to read the instructions, twice, before mastering the starting technique.

I bent over the board, and squeezed . . . nothing.

I re-read the instructions, lifted my left hand a bit higher and tried again.

"Just what do you think you are doing?" came a voice from behind me.

I started. The lumber dropped to the floor with a bang.

"I'm building a tree house," I replied innocently.

He held up the unplugged cord and said, "No you are not."

Before I could protest he asked, "And just where are your safety glasses?"

I should mention that safety glasses are worn at my house, even to change light bulbs.

"I couldn't find them," I answered as I pulled my sunglasses off the table as evidence that I was, in fact safety conscious. "I was wearing these, but they made it too dark to see where I should make the cut. So . . . so, I thought it would be safer to work without them."

He held out his hand and spoke slowly, "Give me the saw."

"But . . . but . . . the tree house . . . we need a tree house," I said.

"The saw. Now," he said using the tone that left no room for discussion.

After that my beloved locked up all the tools and informed me that I was grounded for life. There's talk of padlocking the basement, for my safety, of course.

When Billy's chainsaw threw the chain off the track I understood why I can't have one.

We had determined the apple tree needed a trimming. He was beneath it, arms stretched high above his head, when a terrible metallic screech sounded above the normal roar of metal teeth cutting into wood fiber. A blue-gray plume of smoke erupted from the motor and the chain jumped the track while still rotating. The machine jerked out of control. I watched in horror as the chain flew in the air.

"Lord, please don't let Billy get hurt," I prayed as my hand came to my mouth.

Despite Billy's attempt to control it, gravity won. The chain rotated precariously toward his leg.

Unable to watch, I squeezed my eyes shut.

Billy, who'd kept me at a safe distance, said calmly and without the slightest hint of alarm, "You know, I'm supposed to tighten the chain after running the saw for a while."

I'd just watched a dangerous piece of equipment miss his leg by a fraction of an inch! To him it was no big deal. He acted like these things happen every day. Despite me begging him to take a break, (I needed a moment to collect myself), he retrieved a wrench from the trunk, dismantled the saw and handed me a tool.

"Scrape the junk out of the inside," he said. "I'm supposed to keep this clean. All that gunk mars up in the chain and it won't stay on the track."

I reckon the same concept applies to Skil saws, but I'll never know.

Chapter Nineteen

Pushing Through

"You know there's a whole lotta things in this old world a feller's got to push through."
—Billy Albertson

It seemed like the more vegetables I picked the more there was to harvest. I'd just returned from my parents whose garden was also pulsing with ripe crops. Mother had insisted Dad was incapable of helping her put up beets, so I traveled four hundred miles and spent several days canning beets and every other vegetable that was ready, keeping my mind busy with produce and off the fact her hair was gone, but the cancer remained.

Mother wasn't the only person struggling. Her sister, Della, was losing the fight for her life. She'd been diagnosed with ovarian cancer ten years earlier and had endured every test and treatment doctors at MD Anderson could throw at the disease. She'd taken her poison without complaining, grinding her teeth in pain while silently praying the medicine would work. When chemo was ordered for Mother, they arranged their treatments together and Dad taxied the bald-headed sisters to the doctor several times a week.

I was tired; brain-numb, bone-achy, about-to-break-physically-and emotionally, tired. The visit hadn't gone well. Mother's treatments had zapped her strength, but not her determination. She had worked until she was exhausted, then unleashed her frustration on me. I felt like I couldn't do anything right. She'd barked orders when I didn't gather fast enough and was impatient when I didn't know how to prepare the beets for canning. How could I know what to do? Mom had kept me locked out of the kitchen for forty years while she did all the work. At one point she'd said, "You're going to have to understand this is something I'm going through on my own. You can't help me."

I knew she wasn't talking about the vegetables. There is enough of my mother in me to want to do things myself. I wanted to gather, cook, and prepare the beets under her direction. Not with her standing by my side expending precious energy. I couldn't be much assistance in the process if she was doing most of the work.

I had left in tears feeling like a failure. I was unable to perform simple tasks. Most of all my tears fell because she wasn't well and I couldn't make her better. How could I support her through her treatment if I couldn't properly pull beets from the ground? I was glad to return to Billy's because, like Mother, he needed me; only he never snapped when I screwed up.

And I screwed up all the time.

Instead of selling vegetables, Billy could make a mint renting hiding spaces in his garden. He could post a sign at the edge of the driveway, "escape from your troubles, hourly rates available." He'd have to turn people away.

Billy thought I was helping, but actually I was hiding in the corn, knees deeply embedded in the dirt, picking every bean that was winding around the stalks. While poison dripped into Mother's veins, hot tears bubbled up from the marrow of my bones. She was slowly and excruciatingly battling a deadly disease, and I was powerless to help. As tears dotted the clay I asked God why the cancer had returned. Why do people suffer? Why is life so hard? Why God, why?

When planning a pity party, there is no better place than deep inside the garden. Red clay stained the lines on my hands as I released my tears and sought answers. Sweat dripped as I tossed beans into the bucket, working until the back of my shirt was wet with sweat. I was pushing myself and trying to exhaust myself with something other than worry. As I complained and wondered why I couldn't solve these problems, Jamie approached.

"Billy says you need to take a break," she said.

"Tell him I'm almost done," I said while hiding beneath the bean leaves so she wouldn't see my tears. "I'll be there in a minute."

She left to deliver the message. Two minutes later she returned with a Styrofoam cup of red Gatorade. "Billy sends this and says you really need to get out of the sun," Jamie said.

I took the vile beverage. "Tell Billy I'll be there in two minutes," I said through my teeth.

I wiped my nose on my sleeve and continued. Soon, a shadow covered me.

"You're gonna have a heat stroke out here. Come on in now," Billy demanded.

I didn't want him to witness my emotional breakdown. We sat on his swing, both thankful for the breeze. Billy tapped me on the knee. "I can't have you falling over on my watch you know," he said.

I nodded and pulled my cap down low on my head. "I was out there talking to God, and you disturbed me," I said.

"You know," he said, looking away so I could wipe my nose on my shirtsleeve, "life's not easy. Remember in the Bible the woman who sold everything she had just so she could get to see Jesus? She had to push through a lot of people to get to him, but she got healed." He pointed to the crops and continued, "Take this garden. It's not easy work. You gotta push through the ground and bust it open before planting the seeds. Then you gotta push the tiller through the dirt and lay the rows off so you can plant; then after everything starts growing real good, you walk out there one day and the field is full of weeds."

I nodded. Billy's had his shares of obstacles. At eighteen he cheated death when a slab of wood flew through the air at the sawmill where he worked and embedded in his jaw. A newspaper article quoted Billy's dad saying, "He took it like a man." I assume this means he didn't complain. Billy has worked physically hard all his life. He's raised two children and several herds of goats. He's outlived most of his siblings and has buried a wife. Yet through it all, Billy greets everyone with a smile.

My life has also been a continual weeding process. I've been divorced, a single parent, seen both parents diagnosed with cancer, and overcome a brief bout of cancer myself.

"You know Billy, sometimes I just get tired of pushing," I whined. "Every once in a while I'd like to have it easy."

He tapped my knee and nodded. "Sometimes you gotta push even when you don't want to. When you're as blue as the sky that's when you gotta push the hardest. When the harvest comes, even though you're tired you gotta dig through the vines to find the fruits of your labor. There's many things in life you just gotta push out of your way. But in this life the most important thing is being saved. You gotta know Him," he reminded me.

This was the first time he'd mentioned God, although he didn't have to tell me he was a Christian. I knew that by his actions. I think somewhere the Bible mentions we shall know Christians by their actions. I understood what Billy was saying, but his words didn't lessen my pain. In my heart, I want to handle life's adversities with grace and a smile. I wanted to be like Billy and leave the future in God's hands. I'd like to be able to pray, "God, here I am. Whatever your will is in my life, do it. Keep me from getting in your way and work your perfect plan in my life."

But my human emotions get in the way. I fight a constant battle in my mind, and instead of trusting Him I whine, "Why is this so hard?" I push against His plan for my life. I wonder, if I could manage to get out of my own way for a moment what would God do in my life?

Billy lopes through each day rarely making plans or promises. His motto is, "I don't make no plans. I'll do it, if the Lord is willing." He leaves every aspect of his life in God's hands. If a chicken dies, he figures he had too many. If someone brings a bunny to his door, he figures God saw it fit for him to raise bunnies. It there is no rain, or too much rain, or the wind rips the corn to shreds, he accepts it all as part of God's plan, never once complaining.

On the other hand, I'm "Miss I Can Do It Myself." I try to control the situation. I plan my day from beginning to end, then worry, manage, manipulate, and get upset when things don't go according to my plans. Billy doesn't let life's struggles bother him. He believes God will provide his every need and God has done just that. A feed store allows him to clean out tractor trailers that haul hay. He rakes the excess that has fallen from the bales and uses what others consider worthless hay to feed his critters. The community food bank allows him to take bread that has expired and is no longer fit for human consumption, which he feeds to the goats. People visit bringing food and items he needs for the farm.

When I pulled into his drive on that hot July day, I had no way of knowing that his daughters, Janet and Denise, had prayed God would send help, possibly a Boy Scout troop, to work in the garden. Janet had just moved to North Carolina. Denise owns a small business that keeps her occupied. Neither of us believe it was coincidence that brought Billy and I together. I couldn't have known the Albertson family was praying for help, and I certainly had no idea how much I'd need a friend like Billy.

I've lived in Atlanta for almost ten years, and I can say he is the only true friend I have. Making friends has never been difficult for me. I've always said, "I've never met a stranger." But there is something about people here that are stand-offish. It's almost as if the more I try to befriend someone, the more they question my motive.

Where I was raised, people never visit someone empty handed. An inexpensive token, a flower, vegetable from the garden, or perhaps a book all make perfect gifts. This gesture extends the hand of friendship and shows others that they matter. But today, locked inside safely gated communities and subdivisions, people have become islands to themselves, effectively saying to each other, "No thank you. I have everything I need behind this gate . . . run along now."

The first time I met Billy he looked at me, his blue eyes shining. He had squeezed my hand and stepped inside the personal space we all have. For a moment, my guard went up. But he smiled and revealed a spirit so pure chills pimpled my skin. His expression said, "Welcome home. It's about time you showed up."

And as I sat with him beneath the pecan tree he wordlessly said, "I'm here if you need me." As he pushes through his grief, and I push through my life circumstances, we lean on each other, listen to the chickens, and say a silently prayer of thanksgiving that we have each other.

Chapter Twenty

Making And Partaking of The Spirits

"Oh I reckon a little bit of homemade wine won't hurt nobody."
—Billy Albertson

It was going to be another scorching summer day. I arrived at the farm early, eager to get the gardening chores done before noon, only to find Billy seated at the 60s style Formica table munching away at a sausage biscuit and slurping a cup of strong coffee, acting like we had all the time in the world.

"Have a seat. I'm running a little late," he said while pushing a chair out with his foot. "You want a biscuit?" he asked.

I declined and took a seat at the table. I've never been much of a breakfast eater, and the thought of a sausage biscuit sliding into my stomach with a greasy thud was unappealing.

"Got another busy day ahead," he said between slurps. Crumbs gathered at the corner of his mouth as he poked in the last bite and stood. He retrieved a Good Seasons Italian Dressing bottle from the pantry and placed it on the table. The weathered bottle, milky white with age, contained a deep maroon-colored liquid which I could tell was not salad dressing.

He shuffled to the kitchen cabinet and located two small plastic glasses. I wanted to laugh aloud. My grandma has several "juice glasses" as she calls them, just like Billy's. Quaker oatmeal containers once included drinking glasses nestled inside. These etched glasses also doubled as biscuit cutters. Today, they're still in oatmeal containers, just not Quaker, and now they're made of plastic.

"Have a taste of this," he said while pouring two glasses. He lifted a glass to his lips and downed the contents. "I had my doctor's appointment last week. He asked me if I drank any wine." Billy nodded toward the table. "Go ahead. I made it myself."

I lifted my glass and sniffed. The pungent fruity smell of Concord grapes filled my nose. I took a sip. The rich purple fluid was strong, burning my throat while traveling across my tongue and into my stomach which soon reminded me it was barely eight-thirty in the morning.

He tipped the glass and drained the last drop then said, "I told my doctor I didn't drink wine. But then remembered I have a small taste of homemade wine every now and then. My doctor said, 'Oh a sip of wine every now and then would be good for you.'"

I finished off the contents in my glass and prayed the buzz I felt would wear off before I had to drive home.

"So I've started having a drop or two every morning," he continued as I placed the dirty dishes in the sink. The grapes out back will be ready tomorrow if you want to learn how to make wine."

A woman would have to be a fool to turn down that kind of invitation.

The following morning I arrived, notebook in hand, eager to learn something new. Now before someone reports Billy to the Bureau of Alcohol, Tobacco, and Firearms please know that under Federal law a person is allowed to make up to 200 gallons of homemade wine if it is for personal use and not intended for sale. No laws are being bent, or broken here.

Billy had already picked and cleaned the fruit and removed the stems. "I guess we need to take off our shoes and commence to steppin'" he said while lifting one foot off the floor.

When Billy says those things it's hard to know whether he's joking or being serious.

"Naw, just kiddin.' Our hands will work just fine," he said while placing a wire potato masher in my hand.

And so it began. I guess it was complete stupidity on my part to have worn a good shirt. Soon juice splatters, which looked like blood, covered my white tee shirt. I didn't have to ask, for I knew it was ruined.

"I'm going to the shed," Billy said while placing a five gallon bucket of grapes at my feet. "Back in a jiffy."

Billy returned with a glass gallon jar tucked beneath each arm. Two more jars were pinched between his fingertips. "I figure I can sanitize these here vessels while you mash," he instructed.

So I mashed until I thought I couldn't mash another grape.

"We need to fill these half-way with "pumy," cover them up good, and let them sit for a week," Billy said while I thought, *What in the world is a "pumy?"*

He held his arm straight, then using it as a bulldozer, pushed everything on the kitchen table toward the wall.

"There we go. Now we've got some room to work," he said.

Once we'd filled the jars with mashed grapes (which I figured out he calls "pumy"), he retrieved washcloths and large rubber bands from a drawer. Each jar was covered with cloth and secured with a rubber band.

Billy continued, "This should keep the fruit flies outta our wine. I'll put this in a dark place and cover the jars with a blanket. Every three days I'll hafta stir the grapes. Then in seven days we'll strain this off and add sugar."

Seven days later, wearing my wine making shirt, I was ready to learn step two.

"You know the men of the church found out I had some grape vines and they decided to teach me how to make wine," Billy said while returning from the back of the house with jars of pulpy juice. "This here wine is made like in Jesus' days, without yeast. It's completely natural."

I nodded like I understood. My vast knowledge of wine would fill a thimble.

"Zippy, step outside and fetch me one of those slop buckets," Billy said.

I returned to a table full of jars. Approximately two or three inches of grape peelings had risen to the top, as had the seeds and fruit. The middle layer contained juice. A layer of purple silt had settled at the bottom.

He handed me a wooden spoon then placed a colander inside a well-used plastic bowl.

"I don't like to waste any of this. Put the hulls into the strainer and we'll go from there," Billy said.

I did as told while Billy used a small spoon to release drops of juice that were captured inside the peelings.

"Now, we've squeezed out all the juice. Toss the hulls into the bucket. We'll feed them to the chickens later," he continued.

I scooped the remaining fruit, then poured juice through the colander. Six vessels later, the bowl was full. Working together, he poured while I strained the juice once more through cheesecloth. He placed the empty jar on the table and said, "I'll get the sugar. You slop the chickens."

I stepped out back and dumped the peelings into the chicken lot. The flock erupted in a cacophony of cackles, clucks, and crows. I apologized to the white chickens that stepped under the bucket at the exact moment I began pouring. Feathers flew as they rushed to grab a treat and then find a hiding place to gobble down the snack. In seconds, every peeling had vanished.

I returned to discover Billy standing beside the refrigerator. "Now there's a couple ways we can do the next step. We can add sugar and taste to tell when we've added enough or, we can do the egg test," he said.

Surely he didn't mean break an egg into the juice.

"What do you mean, egg test?" I asked.

He held out a raw egg and said, "Well you take this here egg and put it in the juice. It'll sink to the bottom of the bowl. You add sugar and stir, add more sugar and stir some more. When it floats to the top, you have the perfect amount of sugar."

Now this time I was certain. He was kidding me.

He rinsed the egg and placed it unbroken, still in the shell, into the bowl of unsweetened juice. It sank like the proverbial stone. He placed a wooden spoon in my hand, and grabbed a bag of sugar.

"You stir, I'll pour," he said.

His confidence in me was amazing; I hoped the egg wouldn't crack during this little experiment. I stirred gently, feeling like a complete idiot. Finally, the egg floated to the surface.

"Did you see it?" he asked while pointing to the juice. "It's floated to the top. We're done."

I was amazed.

Billy removed the juice-stained egg. "Reckon this'd kill a feller if he ate it for lunch?" he asked.

I wasn't going to try it, that's for certain.

He returned with two teaspoons which he dipped into the juice as he said, "Give this a taste and tell me what you think."

Oh wow! The juice was tart in a way that tickled my tongue, yet sweet with a rich-bold flavor that tasted like rays of sunlight squeezed from the sky. My face couldn't hide my surprise. I smiled, said nothing, and held out the spoon for a refill . . . just in case the first taste was a fluke.

Billy grinned and said, "Makes you want to slap your grandma, don't it? Now, we've got to pour this juice back into our vessels and put them in the dark. In thirty days we'll have wine," he said with a knowing wink.

He handed me a marker. "You mark it on the calendar so we don't forget when to bottle our brew."

Calling Mother each day had become my routine. I called because I wanted to know how she was handling the chemotherapy and because she has a tendency to lock herself inside the house and ignore the outside world.

"Guess what I learned today?" I announced bravely.

My parents raised me as a Freewill Baptist. I have no idea what that means other than any amount of "freewill" I practiced would result in certain death and immediate arrival in the lake of fire that is hell. Listening to inappropriate music put believers on the path to hell. Sex before marriage, are you kidding me? I'd wake up in hell with Satan for sure! My father's brother was killed by a drunk driver before I was born. Consequently, according to both parents, if freewill included partaking of the spirits, "in any shape, form, or fashion" those who did would suffer an immediate transferal from their house to the dark and fiery pits of hell.

That note alone kept me sober as a teenager, and as an adult.

Because I was safely hundreds of miles away, I shared my wine making experience with her. She listened intently as I described each step, gradually building toward the egg finale.

"You put a real egg in the juice?" she asked.

"Yup. But we didn't break the egg. We added it whole," I replied in a confident tone. After all, my wine making knowledge had vastly increased today. I now knew enough to fill a tastevin. After I had finished the line fell eerily silent. *Here it comes*, I thought. *I'm going to get the business. She's warming up for a sermon. Scripture is going to be quoted.* I cringed as Mother cleared her throat.

"You know your Dad's got a bunch of grapes just hanging on the vine. They're getting ready to go to waste if someone don't put 'em to good use."

"Well, don't let them go to waste," I said. "I'm coming in this weekend. I'll bring them back with me. Billy can use them to make wine. You know, he makes communion wine for church."

That should prevent any sermon perched on her lips.

Then something akin to a Christmas miracle happened. My mother said, "Well, actually I was thinking you could teach me and your daddy how to make wined," she said to my amazement.

I never understood why she called it "wined." But somehow the forbidden fluid was not only allowed, but would soon be prepared in the house where I grew up. I held the phone away from my ear and looked at the receiver. Somehow, my radical religious parents had become spiritualists who partake. And so I began contributing to the delinquency of my parents.

"Uuh, okay . . . sure," I said with a bit of puzzlement in my voice. "But first you're going to need some supplies. You're going to need several wide mouth glass jars."

"Like what pickled pigs feet come in?" Mother said. "I got two of those jars right here." She had moved from the couch to the upstairs pantry. The sound of glass clinking together could be heard along with Dad's voice in the background asking, "Woman, what *are* you doing?"

"Hush up. I can't hear a word she's saying," Mother responded. "Renea's going to teach me how to make wined."

"You're probably going to need more than two jars," I said.

"Larry, you're going to have to take me to the recycling center," she said to Dad. "We need glass jars and empty wined bottles."

That weekend I arrived at my parents with typed instructions and the supplies I thought they'd need to start their own brewery. I lugged everything into the den.

"Whatcha bring all that stuff for?" Mother asked.

"I thought it'd be a good idea to bring everything we'd need," I responded.

Dad spit tobacco juice into a Coke can with a hole cut out of the top. He nodded toward the stairs and said, "Daughter, you might want to have a look upstairs before you unpack."

I followed Mother to the kitchen where I found the table covered with bottles and jars of every imaginable size and color. She skipped around, touching the glassware like they were precious gold. She had Crown Royal, Bacardi, and cheap two dollar gallon wine bottles, of which she was most proud. Her eyes sparkled, and a smile, something I hadn't seen in a while, adorned her face. My mother was happy.

I almost wept with joy.

"Where did you find all these?" I asked.

She held up her hand to stop me. "That ain't all," she said as she pointed toward the door. "Step outside and have a look."

Two wheelbarrows were piled high with bottles. She'd never live long enough to drink the amount of wine it would take to fill all the vessels.

"I figured it'd be a good idea while we were pilfering through the recycling containers to go ahead and get all the wined bottles I might need," Mother said.

Dad had slipped in behind me. "Think we got enough?" he asked.

I laughed and asked, "You got all these at the recycling center?"

The sound of spit splashing inside the metal can signaled the beginning of a story.

"Yup. But we got more than that." He paused for emphasis and said, "We got arrested."

"You got arrested?" I asked, wide eyed.

Dad responded, a bit proudly, "Well not really arrested. But we did get pulled over. You know that woman I married made me take her directly to the recycling center after she got off the phone with you. So we rummaged through there carrying load upon load to the truck. And we almost made it home. We were in the middle of the town square when the blue lights flashed in my rear view mirror."

Mother interrupted, "I said, 'Larry, put on your seat belt.'"

Dad spit again. "And I said, 'Woman, I'm wearing my seat belt, you put yours on.'"

"That Officer Maney sidled up the truck, looked into the back, and said, 'Sir, did you get those at the recycling center?'" Dad said.

Mother punched Dad lightly on the shoulder. "Tell her what you said . . . tell her."

Dad continued, "I said, 'No sir, I didn't get 'em there . . . she did.'"

She pulled the chemo cap from her head. I winced at the sight of her baldness. The she said proudly, "So I yanked my cap off and bared my bald head at him like this. I said, 'I got these here bottles to make me some wined, Doctor's orders.'"

I have created two monsters.

While Dad gathered a second bucket of grapes Mother and I hovered over a bowl rupturing grapes with a potato masher.

"There's got to be a faster way," she said.

131

Once Mother starts something, she likes to be finished speedy quick. She rummaged through the cabinets and to my surprise placed a blender on the counter.

"I bought this years ago to make juice with. Looks like now's as good a time as any to plug her in," she said happily.

Yeah, right. Looked like a well-used Daiquiri maker to me.

Straying from the proven process made me nervous. I believed we shouldn't deviate from Billy's proven methods. After all, he'd been making wine, I mean "wined," for many years.

The whirl of the blender drowned my protest. While my concoction was layered just like Billy's, Mother's floated in a purple froth. Seeds mixed with hull and juice. Technically there was more volume, but I was concerned her wine would be bitter. It seemed logical that seeds that had been split and bruised during the blending process would release a bitter taste. But what did I know? I only knew that it was a bumper year for grapes because Dad just kept 'em coming until it was time for me to return to Georgia.

Meanwhile, back at Billy's winery, things were, according to him, "Comin' right along." To me, our wine looked exactly like it did when we put the jars in the sewing room and covered them with cloth thirty days earlier. That didn't matter, Billy had proclaimed that today was "bottlin' day" so let the bottlin' begin. Professional winemakers call this "racking." Whatever one calls it, the fermentation process was over and it was time for the most important step, we had to taste the recipe once more.

Billy arranged his five jars on the counter beside my lone jar. He placed a well-used coffee cup in my hand and poured. I lifted the cup and inhaled. The delicious aroma of grapes had me licking my lips.

"I prefer homemade wine over gov-mint wine any day," he said while taking a sip.

It was delicious. A dark, rich, sweet wine without the hint of oak, smoke, or preservatives. He then poured liquid from the jar I'd made. I brought the cup to my nose. It smelled like vinegar; it tasted like vinegar.

"Uuh, Billy, I think something's wrong with mine," I said.

"Not possible," he said while pouring a taste for himself. He tossed the purple liquid to the back of this throat and swallowed. After coughing and gasping for air he announced in a hoarse voice, "Naw . . . just needs more sugar."

I guess the egg test didn't work for my batch.

We added more sugar, tasted, and added more, then returned my defective batch to the darkness to work some more.

"I haven't had a single drop of that wined," Mother complained when I called to ask about their bottling day. "I can't keep your dad out of it long enough to pour it into bottles."

"She's telling a story," I heard Dad say in the background. Then they both laughed. A sound that brought stinging-joyous tears to my eyes. I'm happy to announce that Mother's wine was delicious. It was so tasty that Dad drank it straight from the jar. I suspect Mother did too, but she'd never admit it. Right now, their laughter was the only thing that mattered.

The bottles that they risked their reputation to gather were never used.

And despite, or perhaps because of, the added sugar, my wine made a delicious vinegarette.

Chapter Twenty One
Dandelion Wine

"I figure if Billy can make wine, so can I."
—**Renea Winchester**

Remember that catchy little ditty, *Anything you can do, I can do better. I can do anything better than you?* Since I couldn't turn grapes into wine, I was determined to make something Billy couldn't: dandelion wine.

"Why in the world would you want to do that?" Mother asked when I told her about my latest experiment. I think I heard her take a slurp of homemade wine, but I digress.

"Because, it'll be fun. Besides, I like to try new things," I responded.

I'd recently read an article by Spence Johnson in *Back Home Magazine* (March/April 2008), about making dandelion wine. The bottles of brew looked pleasing to the eye. Plus, I try to learn something new everyday. This was about as new as I could get.

According to the article, " . . . it takes a gallon of blossoms to make three gallons of wine."

I would soon discover it takes one million five hundred thousand teeny tiny dandelion blooms to fill a gallon bucket. Finding dandelions isn't as easy as when I was a child. Today's chemically treated over-fertilized lawns are practically devoid of weeds. Years ago, I needed to look no further than my front yard that was adorned with brilliant golden blooms. My parents encouraged the children to pick them; if they weren't picked, they soon transformed into dingy brown puff balls begging for a breeze on which to carry their numerous seeds. While picking flowers was fun, I preferred to scamper through the yard pausing long enough to pluck a handful of puff balls.

But today, in my patchy front lawn I could only find three flowers, a significant stumbling block in wine making until I remembered the golden carpet that lined the sidewalk not far from the house. I took to the streets scouring my favorite rough and tumble outdoor arena, the Target shopping center. I chose this location because last year I had plucked succulent blackberries that were growing wild beneath the all-seeing eye of the security camera. It seemed only natural I would find some dandelions there also.

For the three readers who might be considering making this particular rotgut, let me warn that when pickers are bent over—ass-to-the-sky—gathering the low-growing brightly-colored blooms, be prepared to be honked at . . . often. It's also important to realize that on the very day one decides to pick the fruit of these pollen producing plants, everyone she has ever known will decide that now is the precise moment they need to dash to Target. Additionally, the weather is not likely to cooperate. I soon learned the petals do not open on an overcast day. That didn't deter me. I reasoned the flowers would open once I brought them home and placed them beneath a lamp. The most important task was to collect as many flowers as possible, and not get arrested during the process.

My daughter's school teacher was the first to sound her horn. She caught me mid-bend as I was reaching for a blossom. I waved and smiled. She's a tree-hugger and would understand what I was doing, should I find it necessary to explain my actions. Heck, she might join me. The second was none other than the gossipy church deacon. I encountered him while pacing the sidewalk head-bent looking a bit, shall I say, mentally challenged. I waived an acknowledgment when he tooted the horn, then said a silent prayer of thanksgiving when he didn't stop to chat.

When I realized that someone might report me to the authorities, I developed a plan. I bought a small pack of gum, which in today's world comes with an enormous plastic bag. I then made a grand show of picking up nonexistent trash. I looked directly into passing cars establishing eye contact with the driver, challenging them, hopefully leaving them feeling guilty as to why *they* weren't cleaning up the planet by gathering discarded pieces of invisible trash.

Most of them probably thought, "Isn't that the crazy lady that was foraging in the briars last year like a common hillbilly?"

I gathered as many blossoms as I could find, which, when measured was barely four cups. Adjusting Mr. Johnson's recipe, I used one pound of sugar, a quarter of an orange chopped into chunks, and nine cups of water. Once I had rinsed the flowers, re-rinsed, and then dipped them once more in water to ensure anything icky had vanished, I placed them in a container of heated water, sugar and the orange. I took a sip. It was delicious. Then I sprinkled the mixture with yeast, covered the container, and took it to the upstairs bathroom where it would sit all alone in the dark for three days.

I should probably mention that I did not tell my husband about my little experiment, which was why I hid the concoction in the upstairs bathroom. He's a wine snob drinking only "gov-mint" wine. The entire dandelion experiment would be lost on him.

Three days later it was time for step two. The second step is to remove the blossoms and strain the liquid through cheesecloth. I should also mention this day fell on a day our family was going camping, but I digress.

Camping would be much easier if we could jack up our house and place it on wheels. We seem to pack everything a family of four could possibly need during a 72 hour trip, yet manage to forget crucial items like toilet paper. The list making process begins days in advance, followed by the gradual assembly of items into the kitchen and subsequent stop at the grocery store for Charmin once we're ten miles from home.

Friday morning, I checked the list with the mound of supplies. We'd decided this year to bring one cooler and store each meal in a separate storage compartments with the hope that we wouldn't be rummaging through the cooler looking for ingredients. I had also decided to precook as much as possible, especially foods requiring a lot of cleanup, like bacon and sausage.

I carried the dandelion bucket from its upstairs hiding place, discarded the top layer of blossoms, and strained the liquid into a large glass jar. I knew the wine wasn't ready but couldn't resist the urge to take a small sip.

It tasted terrible, a yeasty-metallic mingling of bitter blossoms and sugar. I re-read the instructions which by the way, failed to mention this undrinkable stage. *I'm just rushing the process*, I assumed, and placed a deflated balloon on the mouth of jar (as instructed in the article) to prevent bugs from entering the concoction. I returned the contraband upstairs ever watchful of the time. The husband would be home soon. I rinsed the bucket I'd been using for my experiment and dried it with a towel.

Around this time Charlie, my large labradoodle, noticed her bowl and a bag of food had been placed near the door as a sign she was going on a trip. She began following my every step, making sure I wouldn't accidentally forget to bring her along.

My mother has always said, "Be sure, your sins will find you out." Translation: I should have known better than to try to hide the wine making from my husband. I heard the garage door open as I stepped out of the kitchen. Charlie, excited that Daddy was home, jumped between my legs. I tripped and fell headlong into the bucket. There was no reaction time only the hollow clang of the handle hitting plastic followed by me saying, "Oh, this is not good."

Immediately my vision began to decrease as the pressure on my face increased. I filled a bag with ice and pressed it to my face, but the damage was done. My eye was swollen shut. Blood dripped from a cut on my nose and pooled beneath my cheek transforming my right side to a lovely grape color. I would like to say my husband rushed to my aid. Well he did until he saw the bucket lying in the floor and asked, "What's that doing here?"

"What's done is done and there's no need to relive it," I responded then began to cry. "I can't go camping now, your friends are going to think you've beat me."

I removed the icepack for emphasis. "Just look at me. By tomorrow morning this is going to look terrible."

As luck would have it my dearest girlfriend called three minutes after my bucket face-plant. She knew I'd been crying the moment I said, "Hello."

"Girl, you know anything about black eyes?" I asked.

"What? What? Why do you need to know about a black eye?" she asked. "Is there something going on? Do I need to come get you? You just say the word and I'll be there."

The questions came fast, leaving no time for explanation. With the beloved standing at my shoulder I couldn't tell her what I'd done, so I said, "I really can't talk about it right now. I need to get more ice."

In hindsight, that wasn't the best choice of words.

"Law'd have mercy," she said. "I'm turning the car around right now. You hang on, I'll be there in a minute." Then "click." She'd hung up.

While my beloved packed the truck, I slipped into the bathroom, dialed my girlfriend, and explained the situation. Beginning with the words, "I do not have a domestic violence situation. I fell into a bucket while making wine." Followed by, "No, I wish I were making this up, but trust me, I am not."

Soon, she was laughing at me as much as I was laughing at myself.

That night, I slept upright, with a frozen sinus mask on my face, hoping the old wives' tale I read on the internet would ease the swelling. It didn't. The next morning my face was purple with red and green blotches. A scab had formed across the bridge of my nose. It was going to be a long, painful weekend filled with a lot of explaining.

"What happened to your face?" my friends obviously asked as we were setting up our tent.

"Where would you like me to begin?" I responded. "You see, it all started when I decided to make some dandelion wine."

Chapter Twenty Two

Cackleberries and Baby Chicks

"Zippy, take this bucket and fetch me the cackleberries."
—Billy Albertson

I reasoned if Billy could sell vegetables from his carport on Hard-scrabble road, he'd make a fortune dabbling in the egg business. There is a demand for organic eggs, which sell for three dollars a dozen. I don't have to be a math whiz to calculate eggs into money.

Billy can recall a time when laying mash (a vitamin rich food fed to egg producing hens) cost less than five dollars for a fifty pound bag. My grandfather used to run a country store. The day chicken feed prices spiked to five dollars and fifty cents a bag he thought folk would, "get out of the chicken business." Now, with the demand for corn as alternative fuel, prices have skyrocketed. Chicken feed is now sixteen dollars per fifty pound bag, which is why I thought the chickens should earn their keep.

Of course Billy's chickens don't lay eggs, they lay cackleberries. I'll admit, the first time he instructed me to "Go to the barn and fetch the cackleberries," I paused to process what he was saying. At the time I was the tow-mater picker and part-time vegetable sacker, not egg harvester. As I walked to the hen house I chuckled. Sometimes Billy has a language all his own. And when the two of us get together, his cadence blends with mine and forms a cacophony few understand.

In order to ensure an adequate supply of eggs, Billy must have a variety of hens whose ages vary. Young hens begin laying eggs when they are ten-months-old. While chickens can live for many years, those one to five-years-old produce the most eggs. Sometime in the spring, hens begin hoarding eggs or "setting." Setting is a term that defines the incubation period from the moment eggs are placed beneath a hen to when they hatch. During this time the hens stop laying. For that reason many farmers don't allow their hens to set. Instead they gather fertilized eggs from the nest and place them in incubators. Billy puts it this way, "They fire Mother Nature and use technology to hatch chicks." The hen will continue laying and the farmer has both fresh eggs and baby chicks.

I nodded, all while thinking, *I will never need to know this much chick-hatching information.*

"I'm trying my hand at the incubator," he announced one afternoon. "Someone gave me one of those contraptions. I've got it plugged up out in the shed."

I nodded while he added, "But I've got a few hens setting, just in case."

While the term "hen party" refers to a gathering of women, I suspect the word originated from poultry observation. The hens were piled on top of each other . . . two, sometimes three to a nest. Their red eyes glared at me. They clucked a low growl-like warning as we approached. Billy dared to insert his hand into the nest, which triggered a noise unlike anything I'd ever heard. Growls, chirps and high-pitched clucks sounded as the hens began arguing who owned the eggs in the nest.

He removed the "extra mothers" and returned each to her own nest saying, "This here is your nest. Get back where you belong." Then he returned his attention to the hen at the bottom of the pile. He placed his hand beneath her. Once again, the clucking became a rapid fire of chirps and snaps. She puffed out her neck feathers, lowered her head and, pecked his hand.

"Aw now," he said in a soothing voice, "you got any babies?"

He lifted the hen from the nest and examined the eggs. By now the rooster had heard the ruckus and decided he should check on his women. He stood to Billy's left. His head cocked slightly, looking from Billy to me who was pressed up hard against the chicken coop with one hand on the door. Billy repeated this pattern cooing, "you got any babies?" while searching under each hen for chicks and making sure all the eggs had a mother hen sitting on the nest.

"I gotta break up this hen party a couple times a day," he explained to me as I nodded.

It's common to discover two hens setting on one nest, clucking to gain the rooster's attention. Some actually force rivals off their eggs. Once Billy notices a hen is setting, he makes sure the nest contains an even number of eggs. Superstition discourages the placement of an odd number. He then waits. Chicks emerge after twenty one days. He removes the newborns from their mothers and places the featherless fur ball safely in his house away from the larger chickens who will steal them from the nest and kill them.

During the spring of 2009, Billy placed approximately thirty eggs in the incubator. He likes to raise chicks in the spring before the summer gardening season explodes with work. Four eggs hatched with the promise of several more during the weekend. There was just one problem, he was scheduled to be out of town the day the eggs were supposed to hatch. Any chicks that emerged would die of starvation if not removed from the incubator. This is where I come in.

Loving baby chicks is part of my DNA. Each year, my father purchases half a dozen chicks from the local feed and seed. My mother raises this brood with all the love a mother hen could possess. As a result, I have a slight bit of knowledge (albeit by observation only) on how to raise poultry. All I needed was a cardboard box, or as Mother calls it, a "pasteboard" box, and two can lids: one for food, the other water.

Billy's instructions were clear. He told me, "I'm leaving at the crack of dawn. I figure if you come over here around dinner time (that's noon), and again before supper (meaning 6 p.m.), and check on things everything will be fine."

Jamie and I arrived at eleven-thirty. Sure enough, a scrawny baby chick stumbled about between the eggs. I placed it in Billy's house with the four other chicks that had hatched the day before. Unfortunately, the larger chicks were unsteady and stepped on the newcomer. Jamie held it while I returned to add water to the incubator. Eggs placed in an incubator require a high level of humidity in order to hatch. While adding water I noticed three other eggs were moving. I also observed an unpleasant odor.

The chicks were having trouble piercing the egg membrane. I imagined they were exhausted and too weak to make the final push into the world. My heart said I should help them by opening a hole in the shell. I placed a quick call to the knower of all things fowl.

"Uuh, Mom, I'm at Billy's and I need help with his chicks," I told her. I explained the situation.

"Under no circumstance should you help," she instructed.

143

"Why not?" I asked.

"I know it's painful to watch, but this is Mother Nature's way of taking care of chicks that may be deformed, or too weak to survive," she responded.

I didn't like this answer. So I peeled away the membrane from one of the eggs figuring there was only one way to find out if she knew what she was talking about. Meanwhile, the chick Jamie was holding was getting weaker. We returned it to the incubator praying Billy would return soon. The chick was still alive during the 6 o'clock shift, but the chicks inside the partially hatched eggs had died. Mom was right. I disposed of the bodies and left Billy a note explaining the tragedy.

Two weeks later, I was thrilled to read the headline, *Chicken Whisperer to Offer Egg-onomic Stimulus Package*. The idea was hatched after some fowl-haters had moved into the neighborhood where Andrew Wordes lives. They reported Wordes, who has chickens as pets, to Code Enforcement. An officer rushed to the scene and promptly ticketed Wordes for having the audacity to keep pet chickens in a residential area. He maintained he'd been keeping poultry on his property for a while, and besides, the city ordinance is vague and doesn't define poultry as "livestock." Then Andy G. Schneider, aka The Chicken Whisperer, got involved as did former Georgia Governor Roy Barnes who was hired as counsel. I'm not sure which gentleman conceived the idea to give away 600 free chickens, but my question was, "where does the line start?"

Since this is America, it should come as no surprise that three seconds after the event was announced, animal rights activists expressed their disapproval. One person complained in a letter to the newspaper that the cost of raising chickens would run, by her calculation, approximately $600. Another questioned the motive for giving away helpless creatures to people who had no experience with poultry. I realize that *some* people might have ulterior motives for their feathered flock, like animal sacrifices, or chicken feet procurement. I mean, *everyone* knows how important chicken feet are in cult-like rituals. Those with the ability to cast spells and hexes must have chicken feet, or so I'm told, but honestly, as I stood in line I didn't see one voodoo princess.

As for the cost, those who complained obviously didn't read the information distributed at the event. A Brooder is the chick's home for the first six weeks. I figured my mother's pasteboard box would be sufficient.

Cost: free. Fancy feeders aren't necessary either. I used a can lid. Cost: free. Food: free. Acworth Feed & Seed, Cherokee Farm Supply, North Fulton Feed & Seed, Standard Feed & Seed, TC Country Feed & Seed, and Tractor Supply Company all generously donated food which was distributed during the event. Estes Hatchery, Little Gem Hatchery, Mt Healthy Hatchery, My Pet Chicken and Randall Burkey all donated the chicks. Unlike the Governments stimulus package, the egg-onomic event wouldn't cost taxpayers trillions of dollars.

I "carried" Billy with me to this stimulating event. The downy chicks peeped with the excitement each new morning brings. They huddled together, a rainbow of breeds: Araucana, Barred Rock, Rhode Island Red, and Silver Laced Wyandottes with no way of knowing how much pleasure they would bring. I shifted my weight from one foot to the other in an attempt to hide my excitement while I waited. I willed the line to move, eager to hold a chick to my face, hide it beneath my hair and listen as it said, "Peep, peep."

Billy doesn't get attached to his critters like I do. I had yet to meet my chicks and already I loved them. While waiting, we met a volunteer from the Atlanta Pet Chicken MeetUp Group. This is a group of people who meet and discuss chicken issues such as: disease prevention and predator control. She announced, like any new mother, that she'd had four new chicks hatch this week.

"Did you hatch them in an incubator?" Billy asked, eager to learn how the process works.

She shook her head and responded, "No, the momma hen hatched them."

Billy thrust his hands into his pockets and said, "Guess Mother Nature knows best."

"I only have a few chickens, so an incubator wasn't worth the expense," she said as she pointed to a man wearing overalls, yellow checked shirt, and matching cap with the words "Chicken Whisperer," emblazoned on it. "I bet he knows all about the incubation process. All I know is someone placed a thermometer under a setting hen and learned it's about 92 degrees under there," she said.

"Well no wonder mine aren't hatching," Billy said. "I have my incubator set at 98 degrees."

We tried to reach the Chicken Whisperer, but there were too many people. Soon the first chick had been given away. The crowd applauded.

Excitement spread as tiny chicks were placed in the hands of new owners. Billy and I left, each grinning and carrying a small peeping cardboard box.

My intent was to give Billy both my chicks. I'm one of those chicken owners who enjoys playing with something but not the hassle of changing shat-upon newspaper. Billy preempted my plan when he said, "Here, take these home."

He thrust his box into my hands and said, "You and Jamie need to raise these. Then when they get big you can bring them back to me."

I shook my head. I was not falling for that trick. I said strongly, "Oh, I couldn't possibly. I just went with you so you could have four baby chicks instead of two." I pushed the box back. "Besides, I don't have a place to raise baby chicks. You keep them."

"Oh no, no, no that wasn't the deal. You need all of them," he countered.

This was going nowhere fast.

I sat on the tailgate and placed the boxes between us and offered a solution. "I'll make you a deal," I said, "you keep your two chicks and I'll keep my two. As soon as Jamie gets tired of them, I'll bring mine to you."

He smiled and agreed. Billy knew that once Jamie got her hands around a fluffy chick she'd never let go. And he was right. Jamie loved the chicks, as did my teenage son. They each claimed ownership of one chick. Jamie named hers Angel, and my son named his Killer.

For the record I have the most wonderful husband in the world. He knew I was taking Billy to the commodity chicken distribution. And despite assurances that I'd come home empty handed, he knew the odds were I'd come home with some cluckers.

Billy's chicks raise themselves. They stay in a box in his living room with a light bulb clamped to the top of the box for warmth. Water and feed are provided for their convenience. They grow and thrive without constant mothering.

For novice-owners like myself, the Chicken Whisperer distributed a handout that provided excellent guidance and clear instructions. On the top of the paper an urgent message read, "Keep an eye on the chick's bottom. Chicks can get "pasty butt," which can lead to constipation and death. If you notice the buildup of waste on the chick's bottom, take a wet paper towel and wipe it away."

Cluck now. I did not sign up for butt wiping duty.

The literature also warned of salmonella, and urged proper hand washing. I knew chicks also need to stay warm. Nature intended them to stay beneath their mother where it is nice and toasty. The first item needed was heat. I placed a lamp inside a plastic storage container. This would serve as temporary housing until the chicks were ready to enter the real world. Then I spooned a couple tablespoons of food into a can lid, added a separate lid for their water, and began what would be several hours of observation. Billy probably used his pamphlet to line the pasteboard box then went on about his business.

With one eye on my peeps and another on the handout, I learned that peep parenting requires a lot of time. Baby chicks don't know how to eat unless shown. I dipped each chick's beak into the water, and waited for them to learn how to drink. Then I showed them the food. Soon tiny bits of food were flying all over the box, as was what I expected . . . poop. I adjusted the lamp, covered their new home with a bed sheet and went about my daily chores. I returned an hour later to find the largest chick in distress. It lay on its side, yellow wings outstretched, beak open, over-heated to the point of collapse.

Note to self: the 100 watt light bulb is too hot, almost fried the baby. I installed a 40 watt bulb, replaced the soiled newspaper, replenished the food and water, and washed my hands.

Concerned that I might burn the house down, my husband insisted I unplug the lamp at night. I argued that if the light had burned all day eight more hours wasn't a danger, but he insisted my peeps sleep in the dark like real chickens. Live poultry inside our house was one thing; waking up to the house ablaze was another. I unplugged the lamp and filled a mayonnaise jar with scalding hot water to keep my children, I mean peeps, warm. They huddled around the jar, each jockeying for the warmest spot.

I awoke at 3:30 concerned that they were cold. I stumbled to the kitchen, heated some water and replaced the jar. At 5:30 I was awake again. "Surely they are hungry," I thought. I began what would be a six-week routine of round-the-clock chick care.

Day three: I visited Billy hoping to convince him to take my chicks. As expected, the novelty had worn off and the children were no longer excited about chicken duty. Raising poultry was consuming a lot of my time. I arrived at Billy's. His car was gone, but the peeping sound was unmistakable. Inside a small box was a just-born, incubator-hatched chick.

One look told me something was terribly wrong. Its feathers were matted, and instead of standing upright, it lay to one side laboring to breathe.

"The dog got to it," Billy's granddaughter, Kristen, said.

God knows that I love all animals, except snakes, but I am really beginning to hate his dogs.

Since Billy believes we should "let Mother Nature take her course," I didn't ask for details. I gathered the injured chick and scratched a note which read, "I've taken the baby chick to my house."

My husband was going to kill me.

The newborn was half the size of my smallest chick. Its tiny feet were cold and trembling. I realized the odds of nursing it back to health were unlikely, but I had to try. I warmed some water, grabbed a handful of cotton balls and began cleaning its sweet little face. What I discovered was grim. Both of the chick's eyes were closed. I didn't know if it was blind, or both eyes were swollen shut because of the attack. What I did know was it needed my tender loving care.

I managed to get a couple drops of water down its beak but forcing food proved impossible the first few hours. I paired it with one of the healthy chicks and wrapped them both in a towel. Soon both were asleep in my lap.

If I thought taking care of healthy chicks was a challenge, caring for the injured was disastrous. The injured chick survived the first night, but the second day came with new difficulties. Without food it would die. I held water-soaked cotton balls on its eyes until they opened, but it couldn't seem to locate the food. I would have to hand-feed it. A syringe was too large. A medicine dropper also failed, and a drinking straw almost drowned the poor creature. I had the bright idea of making cornmeal paste and forcing it down the chick's beak. When that didn't work I used a toothpick. If I timed it just right when the chick opened its mouth to chirp I could poke a couple slivers of food into its mouth, a feat that exhausted me more than the chick. Have you ever tried to balance a grain of corn-meal on a toothpick?

He responded, eagerly accepting the food one microscopic morsel at a time. After he finished he climbed up my arm and hid beneath my hair then went to sleep. His yellow body was not much larger than a puff of cotton. I loved him.

I had determined, through no scientific process that it was a he. I fed him while saying what a "big chicken" he was, assuring him that "one day you're going to be so big, you're going to beat up those bad, bad dogs."

I reported his progress to Billy who politely accepted my updates but warned, "he might not make it." I disagreed, but Billy, using a kind, non-confrontational tone said, "Don't expect to survive him. He might be too far gone."

He didn't know Blue like I did. My Blue was a fighter.

I named him Blue because his eyes were swollen shut. Since my own eye was still healing from the Dandelion wine making debacle, I called myself Black and him Blue. He still required help removing the matted goo from the corner of his eyes. He'd peep, and I'd coo and tell him how strong and brave he was. The other chicks received less attention. Blue was a special needs chick, requiring round-the-clock care. I'd spend all day holding him, passing my love to him as he burrowed into the crook of my arm and waited for me to cover him with a towel. He was my baby. I was his Momma Hen.

Blue responded and on the third day began eating on his own. I was elated. My family gathered around and cheered, actually clapped to watch Blue stand without assistance and eat, then turn awkwardly and drink. At night, he slept inside his own cardboard box, with a bottle of hot water for warmth. By the third day, he was getting better. I was thrilled.

However I should have listened to Billy's warning.

The next morning Blue was dead.

My heart ached. I screamed, "No Blue! You were doing so well."

My sweet peeping Blue had gone from a matted chick covered with dog saliva to a yellow and black puff of hope. Now in his cardboard coffin, his eyes were once again closed, feathers lying flush against his bony body. I wept, large tears filled with defeat and pain. Billy was right, all the power and love I possessed could not "survive him."

Chapter Twenty Three

Corn, Always in Demand

"There's never enough corn."
—Billy Albertson

I had been volunteering in Billy's garden for two months when I learned he leases an additional three acres of land near his home. I'd noticed corn planted in the field, but never in my wildest imagination thought Billy the cultivator. While there is a strong market for corn, the amount of land it takes to grow is hard to come by, especially in the suburbs. Farms everywhere have disappeared, replaced with subdivisions, shopping malls, and coffee shops. Developers often approach Billy offering exorbitant amounts of money for his valuable property. "Get on outta here. You don't have enough money," he responds determined to maintain the only lifestyle he's ever known, despite the encroaching modern development.

I can't help but wonder how different our hectic lives would be if more farmers had decided to stay versus sell.

Billy grows Silver King, a hybrid breed which reaches a height of 84 inches. Most people believe growing corn is easy. Simply scratch out a place in the dirt, toss a couple of kernels into the ground, and a few days later the earth magically yields all one family could ever want. But unlike Jack-And-The-Beanstalk, maturation doesn't occur overnight. Each seed, if it germinates, becomes one stalk of corn. Each stalk develops eighty days after planting and yields only two ears. It takes six stalks and almost three months to produce the dozen ears shoppers see at the grocery store.

During the growing season a variety of fungal and bacterial ailments can afflict the plant: rust, wilt, blight, and smut, to name a few. Critters such as crows, rats, squirrels, and those loveable masked rotund bandits,

151

In the Garden with Billy

the raccoon, often stop to dine on delectable corn. And then there are the insects. One in particular is the saddleback caterpillar, commonly known in these parts as the "packsaddle."

This inch-long worm of death is a brown creature with lime green, saddle-shaped markings on its body (hence the name). It can be found wedged inside stalks of corn safely camouflaged beneath silky tassels. Its evil ears are pricked—assuming it has ears—waiting for the smallest vibration signaling your intention to steal its dinner. Tiny hornlike hairs cover its body and deliver a powerful sting. These hairs stand guard, sensing the slightest movement. If pickers disturb this monster, they will be stung. Even worse, its hairs detach and adhere to the skin. The sound of curse words filling the air will drown out its laughter. Make no mistake! Pickers will scream, and the evil creature will laugh. Ice packs and baking soda paste offer some comfort, but many people get violently ill and exhibit symptoms akin to allergic reactions after being stung.

It is the mere possibly of a packsaddle encounter that causes most farmers to suit up with long sleeved shirts, and leather gloves. Proper attire during harvest is a must, especially for me. If I were going to help, I had to be covered from head to toe. I am severely allergic to corn. My body has a tendency to accumulate vast quantities of hives, and my eyes swell shut when exposed to the stalks. A tidbit of information I'd kept hidden from Billy who needed to pick a truckload with temperatures hovering around 92 degrees. I couldn't become all girly and too delicate to work today when he needed me the most. Corn must be harvested when ready. The delay of just a few hours means the difference between a succulent feast that fills the mouth with sweetness, and gummy-tasteless, chewy corn.

For parents who need help explaining the sex act, let me offer a quick lesson about the birds and the bees. A corn plant contains both male and female parts. Like all plants, its lifespan is focused not on producing delicious sweet corn for us to enjoy, but being fruitful and multiplying. The male part, located at the top of the plant, is called a "tassel." Its job is to attract bees, and small birds which pollinate its flowers. Farmer's refer to this process as "working the corn." The female part of the corn, located on the cob, is called the "silk." The embryo is called "the ear." Humans know this as the most delicious part of the plant. We enjoy it slathered in butter and sprinkled lightly with salt and pepper.

The sex act occurs weeks before an ear is developed. An immature cob contains many eggs. When the time is right, tiny thread-like strands (called silks) emerge from the tip of the husk. Bees visit the tassels and knock pollen onto the silks. The egg is then fertilized. Each strand of silk produces one kernel on a single ear of corn.

I believe, though I'm no botanist, that once the male has released his tassel, he becomes guardian of the ear. Positioned atop the stalk, he sees our approach. I imagine he nudges the stalk beside him and says, "Get a load of the helper. Where'd he find her?" They snicker, their stalks shaking with excitement. One of the males says, "Watch this." He then sends a signal to an army of razor-sharp leaves who patiently wait as I part the stalks and enter, unaware that they are waiting to cut me to shreds.

The setting for many horror films, the cornfield is an unwelcoming place. Even when the noonday sun is high overhead, seven-foot-tall stalks block out the light, leaving one searching for the rare sliver of sun that pierces the darkness. Leaves whisper in the wind as I bump into stalks, jostling bees in the process. Angry at the disturbance, the plant reaches out with rough green fingers, grabbing the only part of my body left unprotected and vulnerable . . . my throat. I clutch at my throat desperate to dislodge the constricting foliage while I wrestle for my very life. I know why I am not welcome on their property, I'm here to harvest what they've spent months to create.

If the crop that Billy has planted, hoed, and fretted over reaches maturity without falling victim to afflictions and vermin, Mother Nature with her fickle moods and dangerously strong temper can reach down on any given summer afternoon and slap an entire field sideways. It happens, more times than one would want to know. Acres of corn lying bent, slightly broken, while farmers walk the rows, scratching their chins trying hard not to mourn hours of hard work that now lies broken before them.

"A farmer's the biggest gambler around," Billy says speaking from experience.

Each year, the Georgia Cooperative Extension Service estimates the price farmers can expect to receive per acre of crop planted. Using 2008 data, farmers without loans (a rarity in today's world) were projected to earn a whopping ninety dollars per acre of corn assuming each acre yields one hundred bushels. Unfortunately, corn stalks, unlike trees, can't withstand Mother Nature's wrath, and once the shallow roots are disturbed the crop often won't produce. Months of hard work and hope for a profit can vanish in a blink. Consumers don't understand these things. They only want their corn immediately, sooner if possible, priced at twelve ears for a dollar, "if you please."

This is one of many reasons why few farmers turn a profit. They work the land because there's a seed planted in their very soul that pulls them like a magnet toward the earth. While people may look at them and see dirt wedged beneath their fingernails, to them clean hands mean hungry families. Around here, when a farmer cuts his hand he bleeds Georgia clay.

So when one of Billy's customers placed her freshly manicured hands on her designer-label covered hips and forgot her polite southern upbringing because the corn she needed was sold out, not only did the sweat trickling down my backside sizzle, my fingers tightened around the hoe I was holding. I wanted to scream, "Take your ass, and your Mercedes to Publix. Can't you see we're working as hard as we can?"

"What do you expect my guests to eat for lunch?" she demanded.

But Billy, whose purpose in life must be providing me with an example of patience said, "These things are out of my control. I plant the seed, but God provides the increase."

His words left me feeling like the scum of the earth. Scratching her eyes out with my dirty nails would be the only thing that'd make me feel better.

I can see I've got a long way to go before I'm like Billy. I'm what you call a work in progress.

As she spun out of the drive, Billy shrugged off her bad attitude and continued bagging tow-maters. "You know, I can't raise enough corn to make everyone happy," he said, simply.

This was the closest Billy would ever come to complaining. He wants to make his customers happy. He plants this particular variety not because it's his favorite, or because it produces more crops, but because they prefer Silver King.

"Sometimes it isn't possible to please everyone," he continued.

His tone was laced with exhaustion. He'd removed his shoes and taken a seat in front of the box fan. I slipped inside the kitchen and retrieved a Gatorade and a Snickers bar. It was break time. The corn we'd spent over an hour harvesting had filled the back of his truck. Twenty minutes after he put up the "corn" sign, we were sold out.

He removed his hat, placed it on his lap, and opened the Snickers. "You know if I had ten acres of corn it wouldn't be enough," he said.

If Billy Albertson had ten acres of corn, I'd be dead.

Chapter Twenty Four
Future Farmers of America

"Kids these days have no idea where their food comes from."
—Billy Albertson

It's no secret that commercial farmers are a dying breed. Land prices are outrageous, crop prices are pitiful. The price for seed and fertilizer are exorbitant; and don't get me started on the price of fuel. It seems that those who work the hardest to feed the world have the least financial reward.

America's food is now being imported from other countries at who knows what cost to the environment and our personal health. I worry and feel pain in my soul when I see once prosperous farms posted with "For Sale" signs. In my heart I want to have enough money to buy struggling farms, work the land and save it for future generations. I wonder, who is going to feed our children in the years to come?

When I was in school, long before No Child Left Behind, vocational classes were taught to those who weren't pursuing college after high school. Believe it or not, every teenager isn't college material. But that's a different topic. Extracurricular classes such as: Future Farmers of America, Future Homemakers of America, and Auto Mechanics were available to those who would graduate high school and immediately join the work force. Now clubs like Model UN, Peace Activist, and the Ping Pong Club are available to students. In the high school my daughter will attend, there is not one single club that encourages youngsters to learn a blue collar trade.

Lord have mercy on our future.

There is a movement in America to return to our "roots" so to speak. Backyard farms and gardens are making a comeback. Even First Lady, Michelle Obama, has a garden. While mine will never look like hers, or

157

Billy's, I do have a garden designed for my lot. Trees restrict the sun, but I have managed to plant tomatoes in every spot that isn't shady. Beans and squash, which require less sun, are growing relatively well on my property. I've failed to grow beets, and for some unknown reason, asparagus won't grow for me either. While I'll never have enough to sell, I do have fresh produce during the summer and up until the first frost.

During the peak of the tomato season, my friends, Doreen and Milton came to visit. They were excited to meet Billy. I'd been talking about my experiences: gushing about the rabbits, goats, and chickens, not to mention the tomatoes. They own a large farm and had recently acquired four chickens. I explained that they needed a goat . . . or ten. In all honesty, I had a plan; I could transport some of Billy's goats to their farm. I reasoned if Billy could sell goats in the suburbs they'd have no problem selling them out in the country. Besides, goats are the cheapest lawnmowers money can buy. I figured the more goats they owned, the less grass they had to cut. We discussed this while walking out back. They examined the fig trees, tools, and of course, the livestock as we searched for Billy.

"Where is he?" Doreen asked, eager to meet the man behind my stories.

"Oh, he's around here somewhere," I answered. "We just can't see him because the crops are so tall."

At this point the tomato plants were almost five feet tall.

"Ho there!" A voice boomed from the middle of the field.

I smiled as I saw the crest of his straw hat. "There he is," I said joyfully.

He was winding orange bailing twine between the tomatoes instead of individually staking each plant.

"Now that's what we need to do," Milton said, referring to Billy's technique.

It's remarkable how Billy teaches people so much about farming without saying a word. Within moments of meeting Billy all were grinning. He has that effect on people.

"Here's a tomato secret you won't learn anywhere else," I said to Doreen. while pointing to a section of plants. "You remember talking about how spindly our tomatoes get? Last week, Billy took the scissors and snipped the sides of the tomatoes. He trimmed them like you would trim a hedge bush."I leaned in and whispered, "I couldn't believe it. I was sure the plants would die. Now just look at them."

158

I could almost see the wheels turning. There would be no tomato cages this year at their farm. Nope. They would be stringing the plants with rope and snipping their plants before the end of the week.

People from all over the world visit Billy's farm. They arrive as strangers; but leave as friends. Many often return to help in the garden. Omar from Ethiopia sat in the living room and told me, "Billy reminds me of my grandfather. Every time I get homesick I visit."

I understand what Omar means.

Jose is another frequent visitor. Once he asked me, "Is he your grandfather?" When I answered, "No," Jose said, "That's because he's *my* grandfather."

I laughed. One can't help but love this wonderful man.

In the fall, Jose, Billy, and I worked together planting the winter crops: mustard, collards, and turnips. Billy's teachings cross all social and economic boundaries.

I've taken many children to the farm, but the one who plucked my heart-string was Michael Hall. Michael is all boy. His knees are scraped. His tan legs covered with a mixture of bug bites and poison ivy. His hair is so blonde it's white, and his eyes, oh those precious portals don't miss a thing.

Baby chicks were the excuse I used to take Michael and his sister Mia, to the farm. "Let's load up and go see how a real farmer works," I said after they expressed interest in my two chickens.

To my surprise they said, "Okay."

I smiled. After all, how many children get the chance to hold a fragile chick or baby goat these days?

How refreshing to view the farm through the eyes of a child. It took a second for Michael to process everything. He stood still for a moment then slowly walked from the goat pasture to the chicken lot, and then the length of the garden. I explained, best I could, the incubation process from egg to chick, while the rooster tried to drown out my voice with his incessant annoying crows.

"That rooster's cool," Michael said.

I explained the spurs on the rooster's feet and cautioned that should he decide to go in the chicken coop he needed to train one eye on the hens, the other on the rooster.

Michael wisely choose to stay outside the coop.

159

"Kids these days have no idea where their food comes from," Billy often says. "It does them good to visit this place and see how things are done."

And he's right, children and many adults are in a word, clueless. Maybe that's why people flock to his little farm. Parents and grandparents alike bring their children in droves. Mothers who home-school their children make field trips to the farm. And regardless of how busy he is, Billy stops what he's doing and answers their questions. Sometimes he even lets them help with the chores saying, "A little work never hurt no one."

I've watched the most hyperactive child sit motionless the moment a helpless chick was placed in their hand. I also know children whose mother's couldn't make them pick up their dirty clothes pitch hay, pluck weeds, and harvest crops until Billy makes them stop for a Gatorade break.

There is just something magical about Billy.

"Everyone in this world wants to feel useful," Billy reminds me. "I make people feel useful."

Michael, Mia, Jamie and I chased and eventually caught a baby goat and carried it to a swing beneath the shade of a pecan tree. You know, it's impossible to swing in the shade without wearing a smile, especially while holding a baby goat. All too soon it was time to go home. Leaving is always a challenge. Billy's place is a time warp. It felt like we'd only been there fifteen minutes. When I looked at my watch two hours had vanished.

"Kids, we've got to load up," I said. "Your parents are going to kill me."

"Please promise me you'll bring me back," Michael said while trudging to the car.

"Yes please," Mia added. "We love it here."

I smiled. I may have converted a future farmer. Or at least sparked an interest in animals, the environment, and possibly land conservation. As much as Americans have progressed, someone still has to feed the world. It doesn't matter how much technology exists, a farmer's work can never be outsourced. Wouldn't it be nice if a kid who visited Billy's farm grew up to be a farmer?

"Of course we'll come back," I said. "You heard Billy. He said you're welcome anytime, and he means it."

Billy hugged each of us as if we belonged to him then returned to his chores. Michael closed the car door. "When you told me we were going to Farmer Billy's I expected to see someone really old," Michael said. "I thought he'd be bent over, and slow. But, he is so full of spirit."

The hair on the back of my neck tingled. I looked at Michael in the rear view mirror and asked, "What do you mean?"

"You know, his spirit . . . can't you see it?" Michael asked innocently.

Tears pooled in my eyes. "Yes, Michael," I whispered, thrilled that Billy had influenced yet another soul. "As a matter of fact I can, but I thought I was the only one."

Chapter Twenty Five

Sharecropping

"Zippy, why don't you make your garden over here this year."

—Billy Albertson

Someone once explained that in order for seeds to produce fruit they must first die. I've often thought about this notion, dying in order to produce fruit. Perhaps it can be said that people are like seeds: hard and wrinkled on the outside, but inside dwells the very essence of life.

Billy Albertson loves his life. He's one of those remarkable souls who wakes each morning and thanks God he's alive and "up and about for another day." Then from the moment his feet touch the floor, until he goes to bed at night, he's waiting for people to walk into his life.

He's waiting for people like myself, whose life was missing something.

It's hard to describe what I was lacking before I met Billy. He possesses not only the gift of being able to grow anything, but more important, he grows relationships. He loves everyone and everything placed in his path. He can take a seed stored in the freezer for years, chunk it in the Georgia clay, cover it with manure and soon a life-sustaining plant appears. He carries baby chicks in his pockets and calls nanny goats "Mother." Somehow, as if by magic, he makes strangers feel like family with a single handshake. He took this gal into his garden and planted a seed of change inside her heart.

Oh, to be like him!

I can't remember the exact moment I realized that I needed to become more like a seed and willing to die to self in order to live a fruitful life, I only know that it did happen.

Somewhere buried in Billy Albertson's garden is the old me. Portions of me dripped into the clay while sweating beside him. While I may never be the caliber of person he is, his influence has changed my life. I have learned to slow down. I have no idea why I was in such a hurry. Looking back, I realize how much of my life I missed by trying to do too much.

After our first growing season together, Billy decided it would be best if I gave up the idea of a garden on my shady property and sharecrop at his place where the sun always shines. I eagerly agreed but still planted tomatoes and cucumbers at my house. There is a joy, a type of euphoria, that comes after a hard day of work. As I collapsed into bed, my bones weary with exhaustion, the heat from my sunburned neck hot on the pillow, I closed my eyes and thanked God for the opportunity to meet Billy. A snapshot of his garden flashed behind my closed lids. The sound of the rooster crowing and the sneezing goat lulled me to sleep. I fell into a peaceful slumber wearing a smile. I awoke sore, but never happier.

I no longer have pretty hands. I have workers hands. They are calloused and freckled from the sun. My nails are stained and torn. Sometimes I examine them and smile at the dirt permanently embedded inside the fingerprint groves. People look at my hands, painted with age spots and think how ugly they are. But they are unable to know the experiences I have shared while digging in the earth. My ears have been sunburned and peeled. My hair has been greasy with sweat and grime. I am no longer the picture of Southern femininity and, frankly, I'm glad.

I used to complain about minor aches and pains. During the time I've known Billy he has never once grumbled about being tired, sore, or hurting. In 2009, Billy was diagnosed with aggressive "prostrate" cancer. I was devastated. I visited the farm wearing a pasted smile, but was crying before I left his driveway. It seemed like everyone I loved was going to be taken from me. But Billy, being the rock that he is, took the news in stride, saying, "I'll give radiation my best shot. If it works, I win. If doesn't, I go home to Jesus and get to see Margie. I'm a winner either way."

I thought, *that's fine for him, but what about me?*

I am a work in process. I'm working to emulate his behavior. While I'm not as patient as he, I recognize my impatient tendencies and am working to become a better person. It is my hope that I heed his example. I constantly strive to make every day better than the one before.

The relationship with my daughter continues to be strained. She's a teenager; I'm a mother fighting to teach a beautiful young lady how to handle life with grace while respecting herself, and others. The television remains disconnected and there is still no texting. She doesn't need to compare her life with what the lie-box broadcasts as reality. She and I are walking the same path my mother and I did; only now the obstacles are many and the path is overgrown with prickly briars and brambles.

My mother will never hear she is free of cancer. No amount of praying or medical advancements will change that reality. Inside her body there will always be at least one cancerous cell. If her blood cooperates, she receives weekly doses of chemotherapy; if it does not, she waits another week and tries again. She'll never be in remission. To use her words, "It is what it is." When I think about it, tears still form.

I used to hate the nonchalant way she uttered that phrase, like she was helpless to change her circumstances. When I'd pour out my heart seeking her advice those words spewed from her mouth: "It is what it is."

I hated those words then, but now realize the truth behind the statement. She couldn't cure cancer. Neither could I. But what I could do, what I hope I did do, was strengthen the relationship we have. Now, Mother and I can handle anything life throws our way, good or bad.

A little bit of good was tossed my way the day I pulled into Billy's driveway. I expected to find baby goats. Instead I found a world time has tried to forget. A world where new trucks aren't necessary and cellphones don't exist. In this world—Billy's world—patched overalls dry on the line and grass clippings are fed to the chickens. Most of all, in Billy's world everyone matters.

I believe the best lesson I've learned from Billy is that "folk matter." When I step outside myself and "see people," when I look into the eyes and heart of a stranger, I find what I'm looking for . . . home. That's the magic of Billy. That's what Billy Albertson did when he shook my hand for the first time. He squeezed my hand, stepped inside my personal space, looked into my heart, and found a home there.

It has taken me a while to figure this out.

While many people look within for happiness, true happiness comes by helping others. People from all walks of life visit Billy's world. I believe each one is seeking something other than fresh tomatoes (though perhaps, like me, they don't know it yet). But when he extends his hand and looks into their eyes, at that moment they know he cares.

I've often said, "When I grow up, I want to be just like Billy." What I really mean is, "When I grow up, I want to make people feel like they are important."

Thankfully, Billy is still "pluggin' along" in his garden, planting tomatoes, raising goats and most of all, making folk matter.

I've got a long way to go before I'm like him. To use Billy's gardening terminology, "I've got a long row to hoe."

I guess I best get busy. I've got a lot of growing to do before I'm big enough to wear his overalls.

A conversation with Renea Winchester

Q: Some people might look at the title *In the Garden with Billy: Lessons About Life, Love, and Tomatoes* and think this is a book about gardening, but it isn't, is it?

A: We've all heard the phrase, "you can't judge a book by the cover," the same can be said about titles. While the book does contain many stories about the time I spent "in the garden," ultimately it is about relationships and overcoming obstacles. *In the Garden with Billy* is about a mismatched pair — Billy Albertson and I — and the intricate myriad of experiences we've shared. When I met him I had no idea that his wife had just passed. He didn't know my mother was ill, but together we helped each other and harvested delicious vegetables along the way. Billy also introduced me to many new friends. It is because of him that I now teach creative writing classes in nursing homes and assisted living facilities. People matter. Stories matter. Everyone matters.

Q: It sounds like Billy spends a lot of time outside working on his property. How was it possible to drive past his house daily and never see him?

A: I was in my own little world and too self-involved. Billy works outside all the time. Looking back, I did see him once at the bank. He was at the drive-thru teller window. He not only made a monetary deposit, he also included a "sack of tow-maders." I remember because the teller turned to a co-worker and said, "I just love him." A couple years later I had the pleasure of loving him as well.

Q: What made you return to the farm just hours after meeting Billy?

A: That's an excellent question and one I have trouble answering. Initially, my daughter was the reason I returned, but when I met him there was an inexplicable magic that made me want to become part of something bigger than myself. I believe we're our best when helping others. When I tell people about my friendship with Billy, they nod politely and ask, "what is so exciting about working in the hot sun without pay?" My response is to take them to the Billy's. Without fail, everyone I've introduced to him says the same thing, "I love him!"

Q: The phrase, "death is a part of life," is something your mother and grandmother offer as comfort when you experience loss. Can you explain the phrase?

A: Their words may sound crass, but that isn't their intent. It's true: death is a part of life . . . a part I struggle with. I form strong attachments. From trees, to pets . . . friends to family, everything in my life feeds my spirit. When I lose someone, I experience physical pain. A battle is waged within my soul. It is a battle of memories and longing for someone whom I will miss forever. I don't like the finality of death, but prefer to experience smiles, hugs, and love.

Q: What was the most important lesson Billy taught you?

A: Oh, that's easy: Billy taught me that everyone matters.

Q: What's next for Billy Albertson and Renea Winchester?

A: There's always something happening at Billy's. He's slowed down a bit after "fighting that cancer," but he'll never stop gardening. Gardening is his lifeblood. As for me, I've got big plans. I'm going to borrow a goat and sneak it over to my house for "all natural weed control," (don't tell my husband) then I'm going to take a group of kids over to Billy's and give them each a bucket of paint and a brush, and we're going to paint his barn every color of the rainbow. Visit blogthefarm .wordpress to see what's happening on Billy's "little strip of land."

Reading Group Questions and Topics for Discussion

1. Do you think you would enjoy having Billy Albertson for a neighbor? Why or why not?

2. Did reading *In the Garden with Billy: Lessons of Life, Love, and Tomatoes* make you feel differently about farmers and locally grown produce?

3. What is your thought about commercial and residential development and the disappearance of farmland throughout the United States?

4. Do you feel Renea should have spent more time with her mother and less with Billy?

5. Do you believe homeowners should be allowed to keep goats and chickens as pets, or do you think these animals should be classified as livestock and banned from residential neighborhoods?

6. Do you live in a subdivision? If so, would you like to see Homeowners Association restrictions modified to allow vegetable gardens?

7. Were you surprised to read that Billy has traveled out of the country? Where would you take Billy if given the chance?

8. Billy doesn't own a cell phone and Renea no longer watches television. She doesn't "text" or "twitter" either. Has the author's stance on technology made you reconsider the way you use it? If so, how?

9. Renea's relationship with Billy began after she returned to help him in his garden. Would you have done the same? Why or why not?

10. Do you believe their meeting was a coincidence? Why or why not?

Also by Renea Winchester, *Stress-free Marketing: Practical Advice for the Newly Published Author*

Is it time to release your first book? Do you need to increase book sales? Are you intimidated at the thought of marketing your book?

RENEA WINCHESTER

Award-winning Author of
In the Garden With Billy:
Lessons about Life, Love & Tomatoes

While promoting *In the Garden with Billy,* Renea met authors who were struggling to sell their books. Many were victims of well-known-yet unscrupulous-printing companies that charged exorbitant rates to print books the authors could not sell.

Stress-free Marketing: Practical Advice for the Newly Published Author is available at Independent Bookstores and online both in paper, and in electronic format.

For the latest tips, subscribe to Renea's blog
http://adviceforauthors.wordpress.com